The A

Blending

By Anton Swanepoel

Author @ Divetech Grand Cayman.
Photo taken by Steve Tippetts

Kindle ASIN B004ZFTBQ
Print ISBN-1463714181
Print ISBN-978-1463714185
www.antonswanepoelbooks.com
http://www.facebook.com/AuthorAntonSwanepoel

Introduction

Gas blending is a bit like making fudge. One day everything just goes smoothly, and the next day all you end up with is toffee. It is as much art as it is science. Like everything in life, the more you know about it and the more you practice it the better you are at it.

This book is for any person that has an interest in gas blending, deep or technical diving. Even existing gas blenders will find the tips and formulas of great value. Alternatively, a new way of explaining things might just be what is needed to help you understand how gas blending works. Deep and technical divers will benefit by knowing more about the gasses they breathe and the effects it has on the body. In addition to knowing more about how the mixtures they dive with is made, it can also help you plan your dives better for repetitive dives with top up mixes.

From the basics of blending Enriched Air Nitrox (EANx) to Tri-Mix, Helair to Heliox blending is covered.

Additionally included is blending with impure helium (helium that has Oxygen mixed in it, or industrial Oxygen) to formulas on working out the actual breathing mix in a rebreather loop at any depth at any PPO2, and what would be the appropriate mix to bailout to at depth.

Blending to help prevent ICD is covered. This is switching from a high inert gas to a low inert gas. Say from a high helium mix to a low helium mix or a mix that has no helium in. The possibility exists for getting decompression sickness at depth when making the switch.

At the end of the book a chart section is included. These cover standard mixes, for both Nitrox and Tri-Mix. You can use the charts to easily locate a blend and use the values provided to blend your gas. Best gas Charts for Nitrox and Tri-Mix are also included.

This book is a must have for any blender or technical diver, it will be an excellent companion and reference guide. Forgot a formula or need a quick refresher? No problem, just quickly scan the summary at the end of the chapter that deals with the gas that you need to blend. Each chapter is followed by examples to help you understand and learn. There is a question section following the end of each chapter, with answers and workings in the end of the book. There is also a section on tips and tricks for blending at the end of chapters to help you along.

This book is also a companion book to 'Gas blender program, create your own blender program in Excel' www.antonswanepoelbooks.com/gas_blender_program.php, which shows you step by step how to create an Excel spreadsheet that can run on iPhones, laptops, cell phones, iPads and more, blending on the move at your fingertips. You can also mail the author your receipt if purchasing the gas blender book to have a ready made spreadsheet mailed to you. Saving you the time to do it yourself, but with the benefit of being able to change it to your liking.

About the Author

IANTD Komati Springs South Africa.
Photo taken by Andre` Shirley.
www.iantd.co.za

Anton Swanepoel is a diving instructor for IANTD, TDI, NAUI, and PADI. He is a Tri-Mix instructor and a Tri-Mix gas blender instructor. He has a passion for wreck, cave and deep diving.

Although he dives both CCR and OC, his passion is in OC. Working as a technical instructor in a busy dive center in the Caribbean, he gets to live his passion. He has dove OC in excess of 400 ft and loves to share his passion with all.

Table of Contents

Chapter 1

Getting to know the gasses

Air:

Contents: .... 20.95% Oxygen O_2 (rounded to 21%)
78.08% Nitrogen N_2 (rounded to 79%, to include trace gasses)
0.93% Argon Ar
0.03% Carbon dioxide CO_2
0.01% Trace gasses and vapor
Density .... 1.293 g/l
Total molecular mass .... 28.97 kg/kmol

Air is the most common gas used for diving, and until the use of Tri-Mix gas as a diving gas, air was used for deep dives in excess of 500 ft (151,51 m).

Although air is the most common gas used in recreational diving, it is in most cases not the ideal gas. Due to the high nitrogen content in air, enriched air is in most cases a better option.

Deep air diving is still practiced in some parts of the world where it is difficult or impractical to obtain enriched air or other breathing gasses.

Oxygen:

Atomic Number 8
Symbol on periodic table .. O
Atomic weight 15.9994
Melting Point .... - 361.82 °F
Boiling Point .... - 297.31 °F
Density .... 1.429 g/L
Narcosis level .... 1.7 of Nitrogen
(Normally calculated as 1 for ease of calculation)
Heat conductivity .... 26.4 mW/m (milli watts per m)

Oxygen is pale blue, odorless and tasteless when in gas form.

Discovered by Carl Wilhelm Scheele in Uppsala at around 1773, and named by Antoine Lavoisier in 1777.

Oxygen is an abundant element on earth, making up 49.2% of the earth's crust by mass, and is the third most abundant element in the universe.

Oxygen is widely used in the medical field. As a main component of life, supplemental Oxygen is widely given as treatment. Supplemental Oxygen increases the level of Oxygen in the blood and tissue and also decreases resistance to blood flow in many lung diseases. Oxygen is used in hyperbaric treatment of cancer, burn victims, gas gangrene, CO poisoning and decompression sickness, to name a few.

Oxygen is also widely used in industrial processes like metal cutting and melting. Liquid Oxygen is also used in large rockets as an oxidizer.

In aviation and space flight Oxygen is used as a breathing gas due to the low surrounding pressure.

In many armored vehicles, Oxygen is used as a positive pressure gas to help protect the occupants from toxic gas attacks.

Oxygen under elevated pressures can become toxic. Partial pressure exposure to more than 160 KPa or about 1.6 ata can result in convulsions. However, breathing Oxygen at partial pressures above 60 KPa or around 0.6 ata for extended periods can result in permanent pulmonary fibrosis. The alveoli in the lungs start to dry out and their ability to transfer gas in and out declines. High PPO2 over a short time can result in CNS toxicity which symptoms include muscle convulsions, visual disturbances, nausea, twitching (normally in facial muscles), ears ringing, and irritability.

Long exposures over 0.5 ata can result in damage to the lungs and difficulty breathing, to permanent lung damage. To track the Oxygen exposure one must track both CNS toxicity and OTU or UPTD. An OTU (Oxygen tolerance unit) or UPDT (unit of pulmonary toxic dose) is basically breathing 1 PPO2 for 1 minute. But it is not a sliding scale as 1.3 PPO2 is not equal to 1.3 OTU.

Even at long decompression stops on high PPO2, vassal constriction followed by pulmonary edema occurs and both breathing and off-gassing is affected. Many divers elect to decompress on EAN70 to EAN80. Or divers will take air breaks of about 5 minutes on air every 20 to 25 minutes of O2 decompression. (Some do 2 minute breaks every 12 minutes of O2 decompression.)

When diving on a rebreather on long dives, many divers elect to keep the PPO2 low at 1 to 1.3. However it can be needed to drop the PPO2 below 0.7 on long decompression stops, helping the body to more effectively off-gas.

Free radicals are a natural by-product of metabolism. These free radicals have unpaired electrons and can be + or – charged and are highly chemically reactive, damaging cells in the body. The body can cope with the normal level found from day to day activity.

Elevation of partial pressures of Oxygen results in an elevation of free radicals found in the body. At partial pressures above 0.5 ata, the body generally cannot cope with the amount of damage done by the free radicals. The repair process slowly starts to lag and given enough time, permanent damage can result. This is the reason for the exposure time limits to elevated partial pressure of Oxygen.

Here is a short exposure table:

PPO2	Max time in minutes
0.6	720
0.7	570
0.8	450
0.9	360
1	300
1.1	240
1.2	210
1.25	195
1.3	180
1.35	165
1.4	150
1.45	135
1.5	120
1.55	82
1.6	45

Oxygen does not combust itself. However, in the presence of high amounts of Oxygen, it promotes rapid combustion to other materials.

Normal Oxygen partial pressure is 0.20 to 0.21 ata at sea level. A partial pressure below this point is known as hypoxic. Below 0.16 ata signs and symptoms of hypoxia start to show and below 0.1 ata unconsciousness and death can result.

The general range for diving O2PP is 0.16 to 1.6 ata, although it can go as high as 2 ata in hyperbaric therapy.

Although Oxygen has a narcosis level of 1.7 times nitrogen, it is generally taken as 1 when computing END (equivalent narcotic depth) values. This is more for simplicity of calculation and due to the Oxygen level being normally less than the original level as in hypoxic mixes.

When filling Oxygen tanks or blending with pure Oxygen, care need to be taken for the rate of filling and the temperature the tanks reach when filling. A general rule is about 72 psi (5 bar) per minute or slower. Open all valves slowly to reduce the risk of adiabatic compression pressure combustion. This is when a high pressure gas (from the tank or line) enters a low pressure area with speed and hits a dead end (like the end of a pressure gauge). Impurities in the line can ignite due to the extreme temperatures reached, sometimes in excess of 800 °F (426.67 °C).

O2 rebreather tanks being filled at a gas blending station
Divetech Cayman Islands.

Helium:

Atomic Number 2
Symbol on periodic table .. He
Atomic weight 4.002602
Melting Point .... - 457.96 °F
Boiling Point .... - 452.07 °F
Density .... 0.1786 g/L
Narcosis level .... 0.235 of nitrogen

Helium is colorless, odorless, tasteless, non-toxic, inert when in gas form. Astronomers Jules Janssen and Norman Lockyer observed a yellow spectral line signature in a solar eclipse in 1868. Lockyer proposed that the line is from a new element and called it helium.

Helium is the second most abundant element in the universe and is normally only found in gas form, unless in extreme conditions. Helium is found in natural gas fields, with the United States being the largest supplier of helium gas. Helium is the second lightest element in the periodic table.

Helium is the lightest noble gas on earth. Noble gasses are a group of six gasses that are inert and rare, belonging to group 18 of the periodic table and have similar chemical properties, being generally stable, non reactive and rarely found in combination with other elements. Neon, argon, krypton, xenon and radon are all noble gasses.

Helium is widely used in commercial diving due to its low density and low narcosis level, and as a protective atmosphere in arc welding and is used in cryogenics for cooling. It is also used in the growing of crystals to make silicon wafers.

Most of the helium that was present when earth formed has escaped into space, due to the lightness of helium gas. The result is that helium is a rare gas on earth today. The helium found today is mostly from the natural radioactive decay of heavy radioactive elements such as thorium and uranium.

Helium is normally trapped with other gasses in low concentrations of up to 7% by volume. Using fractional distillation, a commercial low-temperature separation process, pure helium can be extracted.

Breathing pure helium can lead to asphyxia and death. The helium found in balloons is required by many countries to have 20% Oxygen in the mix. A common party trick is to breathe the gas from the helium filled balloons to create a Donald Duck voice effect.

Few people realize that helium is in fact narcotic. This is due to the low narcosis of helium. Helium only starts to show in calculations at a greater percentage (normally above 50%) and at greater depth (normally below 250 ft). Helium's diffusion speed is around 2.7 times faster than nitrogen.

Another problem with helium and deep diving is that helium removes heat from the diver's body on deep dives. Put another way, helium has greater heat conductivity and each helium molecule can carry more heat away than nitrogen molecules. But, there are fewer molecules per volume of gas compared to nitrogen, so the effect is only noted when the pressure goes up and sufficiently increases the density of the gas.

Commercial divers get around this problem by heating the breathing gas, but technical divers do not normally have this option.

Divers at shallower depths, around 200 to 300 ft (60 to 90 m), may report feeling colder than on a deep air dive, but this is believed to be due to the narcosis level of deep air dives. The helium density at this depth is not normally enough to chill the diver, the diver is just more aware of the cold when breathing a helium mix rather than air.

The critical depth is normally in the range of 825 to 924 ft (250 to 280 m). This is the range where the helium in the mix removes more heat than the body is capable of producing.

On deep saturation dives, the gas is normally heated to around 86 °F (30 °C) to keep the divers warm.

Helium does not dissolve at the same rate as nitrogen into your tissue due to it being less soluble than nitrogen. However, being a thinner gas, the helium that does dissolve into your tissue does so faster than nitrogen. In short, helium is more diffusible than nitrogen but less soluble. All in all, helium has 2.645 times faster half times (M value) than nitrogen.

Due to the faster half life of helium, decompression for short deep dives (bounce dives) on helium can be longer than if no helium was used. This is due to the fast on-gassing of the helium in a short time. However, for saturation diving, the decompression on helium mixtures would then be shorter as compared to if no helium was used. This is due to the helium off-gassing faster and the fact that less helium dissolved into the tissue. For the normal technical diver the dives we do are mostly seen as bounce dives or short deep dives. This is why some people still prefer deep air dives, as the decompression can be less than that of a helium mixture dive, and calculations are simpler.

Another problem with deep helium dives is HPNS (high pressure nervous syndrome). The believed is that the surrounding pressure that the diver is at is the actual problem and not the helium in the mix. The helium does not have the same effect on the lipid cells as nitrogen and does not cause them to swell out or expand as much. With high helium mixtures and depths in excess of 500 ft, it is believed that the pressure at these depths starts to compress the lipid cells so much as to interfere with brain and muscle signals.

Divers may experience muscle twitching, micro sleep, memory problems, and visual problems, to name a few. By adding nitrogen into the mix (about 5 to 10%) helps keep the problem under control.

Tanks to be filled.
IANTD Komati springs South Africa.

Nitrogen:

Atomic Number 7
Symbol on periodic table .. N
Atomic weight 14.00674
Melting Point .... - 346.00 °F
Boiling Point .... - 320.33 °F
Density .... 1.251 g/L
Narcosis level 1
Heat conductivity .... 25.9 mW/m

Nitrogen is colorless, odorless, tasteless, and mostly inert when in gas form. Daniel Rutherford is credited with the discovery of nitrogen in 1772 and called it noxious air or fixed air when he discovered that it does not support combustion.

French chemist Jean Antoine Chaptal named the gas nitrogène in 1790, and in 1794 the word nitrogen was derived from this.

Nitrogen is very abundant on earth and forms the single largest component in air. Nitrogen is normally very un-reactive at standard temperatures and pressures; it does react spontaneously with a few reagents however.

Nitrogen is resilient to acids as well as oxidants and most reductants. When nitrogen spontaneously reacts with a reagent it is called nitrogen fixation. When nitrogen reacts with lithium the lithium burns to give lithium nitride, and when nitrogen reacts with magnesium it forms magnesium nitride.

Strangely, nitrogen is used in some beer making and is preferred over CO2 due to the smaller bubbles it produces which results in a smoother beer. Liquid nitrogen is used in cryogenics and can be used as a refrigerant in both liquid and solid form. In solid form it looks closely the same as dry ice produced from CO2.

In the medical field it is used to remove warts and cysts, and in the industrial field it is used in the cooling of certain laboratory equipment and super computers.

In diving, nitrogen causes narcosis and is thought to play a major role in decompression sickness. For more information on how dive computers calculate on- and off-gassing including decompression, deep stops and the use of gradient factors see. 'Dive Computers' by Anton Swanepoel
www.antonswanepoelbooks.com/dive_computers.php

Nitrogen narcosis is normally only noted at depths greater than 100 ft, but has been seen in people at shallower depths. When diving beyond 130 ft it is seen as outside recreational diving. Training for deep air diving up to 180 ft in technical diving exists; two agencies that offer this training are IANTD and TDI. (Technical diver and Extended range, respectively).

The deepest depth accepted when diving on air is normally 218 ft due to the Oxygen in air reaching 1.6 PPO2 at this depth. Although many people have gone deeper on air, it is not recommended due to the extreme narcosis, O2 toxicity and the possibility of deep water blackout.

The general thought is that nitrogen narcosis is caused by the nitrogen gas dissolving into the lipid bi-layer of cell membranes which at elevated pressures interferes with the neurotransmitter receptors and protein mechanisms of the cells (mostly spinal column and brain cells). The reason seems to be that the nitrogen under pressure causes the cells to swell up and short circuit signals sent between the brain and the rest of the body. A signal sent to your hand to press the power inflator button to stop your descend may reach your left little toe, confusing it like a chameleon is in M & M packet, not only has he got all the colors but he is sweet as well. ☺

It takes only one to two minutes for the ambient pressure in the brain to reach that of the pressure in the lungs. This will produce a small delay in narcosis if one descends very quickly and is the main reason for that feeling of someone closing the door on you when doing rapid descents. Rapid descents can potentiate nitrogen narcosis due to CO2 retention, especially if the diver did a hard swim before descending without a rest to clear out the excess CO2 that was built up in the swim.

Nitrogen narcosis signs

33 ft and above there are almost no symptoms to detect.

33 to 100 ft one might have mild impairment of thought and reasoning, and a mild feeling of euphoria.

100 to 165 ft motor skills are more affected and the ability to do calculations and make decisions is impaired. The effect of fixating on one idea is present, like only watching your depth gauge. The diver might experience a sense of well being and could become over confident in his/her diving abilities leading to major risk-taking decisions, or the diver may experience the flip side to this and the feeling of impending doom and panic may overwhelm the diver.

165 to 230 ft a diver can become sleepy and judgment is heavily impaired. Simple motor skills are severely affected and delayed reactions are noted, making it difficult for the diver to focus on the dive plan, gas consumption, time, depth and coming back. Insensitivity to body signals such as being cold may occur that could lead to hypothermia without the diver knowing he/she is cold. The breathing may slow down that saves gas and many divers are amazed at how low their breathing rate is on deep air dives; however this can lead to CO2 build up and CO2 poisoning. Hallucinations, hysteria and dizziness may occur and if the diver does not ascend at this point he/she may not come back.

230 to 300 ft loss of memory and mental confusion occur in most divers, and dexterity and judgment are heavily affected. The diver has extreme difficulty concentrating on keeping track of multiple tasks and normally only fixates on one, such as depth, forgetting gas supply and dive time. It takes great concentration and mental focus to follow multiple tasks at this depth at one time.

300 to 500ft heavy hallucinations and dizziness occur, with a very strong sense of impending doom and impending blackout. The diver can lose the sense of time and space and not know where they are. Unconsciousness and death are a very strong possibility in most divers. Even if the diver ascends at this point narcosis will still affect them for some time and the diver may blackout on the way up.

500 ft and below the possibility for blackout is extreme and almost certain in most divers. Dan Manion holds the record at 509 feet (155 m) on air set in 1994. Successful dives by others deeper than 400 ft on air are documented, however more deaths have occurred than successes and one death is one too many. Due to the availability of Tri-Mix, doing deep air diving below 220 ft is highly discouraged and very rarely done these days.

Nitrogen narcosis varies from diver to diver and from dive to dive. You do not build up a tolerance to nitrogen narcosis; your body just becomes accustomed to operating in a state of narcosis and mostly operates by muscle memory (doing a skill repeatedly). Thus, any poorly learned skills will be hard to remember and complicated dive plans will be difficult to follow or remember. Diving habits good or bad will automatically be done and can either save or kill you. Slowing down your actions and staying calm will help you in completing tasks easier while under narcosis.

There are several things that can elevate the effects of nitrogen narcosis you will experience. These include but are not limited to, the speed of your descent, excess CO2 left in the body before descent, CO2 build up (skip breathing or natural CO2 retention), mental state of diver, certain drugs, caffeine, stress, alcohol, fatigue, hard work underwater (swimming hard against a current), negative attitude, and diving outside your knowledge, training and comfort zone.

It should be noted that to discourage deep air record attempts, the Guinness World Records ceased to publish records on deep air dives. The current recorded records are:

1947 Frédéric Dumas, 307 feet (94 m)
1959 Ennie Falco, 435 feet (132 m) (not verified)
1965 Tom Mount and Frank Martz, 360 feet (110 m)
1967 Hal Watts and AJ Muns, 390 feet (119 m)
1968 Neil Watson and John Gruener, 437 feet (133 m)
1990 Bret Gilliam, 452 feet (137 m) (Gilliam remained functional at depth, being able to complete maths problems and answer questions written on a slate beforehand).
1993 Bret Gilliam, 475 feet (144 m), again reporting not being affected by nitrogen narcosis or Oxygen toxicity.
1994 Dan Manion, 509 feet (155 m), (current record) (Manion reported being almost completely incapacitated by narcosis).

Author @ 200 ft, Helium in his mix making it possible to think correctly.
Carrie Lee Wreck, Grand Cayman, Cayman Islands.
Photo taken by Steve Newman.
www.choochoodive.com

Argon:

Atomic Number 18
Symbol on periodic table .. Ar
Atomic weight 39.948
Melting Point .... - 308.83 °F
Boiling Point .... - 302.53 °F
Density .... 1.784 g/L
Narcosis level .... 2.326 of nitrogen

Argon is the third most common gas in the earth's atmosphere and the third lightest noble gas. Most argon found today is from the decay of potassium 40 in the earth's crust. Argon is derived from the Greek word αργον meaning "lazy" or "the inactive one" and is due to the element's nature of undergoing almost no chemical reactions.

Industrially argon is produced by the fractional distillation of liquid air.

Argon was first suspected by Henry Cavendish in 1785 but it was not until 1894 that Lord Rayleigh and Sir William Ramsay in Scotland isolated the gas from air.

The gas is mostly used as a shielding gas in welding and other high-temperature industrial processes today due to its low reactivity. Argon is also used in incandescent and fluorescent lighting and other types of gas discharge tubes.

In diving argon is mainly used as an insulator due to the thickness of the gas; a small pony bottle of argon is normally carried and attached to the dry suit inflator. However, this can in some cases cause skin bend symptoms (Argon is twice as soluble as N2) as the argon enters the body through the skin; however these are usually only mild and resolve quickly after exiting the water.

Diver returning from a deep cave dive. Note argon cylinder on side used for dry suit inflation.
IANTD Komati Springs, South Africa.
Photo taken by Andre` Shirley.

Neon:

Atomic Number 10
Symbol on periodic table .. Ne
Atomic weight 20.1797
Melting Point .... - 415.46 °F
Boiling Point .... - 410.94 °F
Density .... 0.9002 g/l
Narcosis level .... 0.274 of nitrogen

Neon is the second lightest noble gas and has the narrowest liquid range of −415.21 °F to −410.71 °F. Per volume it has over 40 times the refrigerating capacity of liquid helium and three times that of liquid nitrogen, making it an excellent refrigerant choice if you can afford the price.

Neon was discovered by the British chemists, Sir William Ramsay (1852–1916) and Morris W. Travers (1872–1961) in London, in 1898. Ramsay chilled a sample of the atmosphere until it became a liquid and then warmed the liquid while capturing the gases as they boiled off. Neon was one of the gasses that boiled off from the experiment and its discovery was made.

Although neon is the fifth most abundant element by mass in the universe it is rare on earth and only found as a trace element in air. Neon is commercially extracted from air and mostly used today in lighting tubes. This started to replace the nitrogen lighting tubes in 1910 for most signs as helium glows reddish orange, making it a different sign from other noble gas lighting tubes.

Neon is also used in television sets, wave meter tubes and as a commercial cryogenic refrigerant. Neon however is very expensive and can be up to 60 times the price of helium depending on the quantity bought. In diving, it is mostly used in deep saturation commercial diving.

Like helium, neon is less narcotic than nitrogen, however unlike helium, neon does not distort the diver's voice and a voice scrambler is not needed to correct the diver's voice. Although few experimental deep dives have been made on neon, the dives that were done showed similar narcosis levels as Helium.

Hydrogen:

Atomic Number 1
Symbol on periodic table .. H or H2 for hydrogen gas
Atomic weight 1.00794
Melting Point .... - 434.45 °F
Boiling Point .... - 423.17 °F
Density .... 0.08988 g/L
Narcosis level .... 0.541 of nitrogen

Hydrogen is the lightest and most abundant chemical element found in the universe and forms roughly 75% of the chemical elemental mass of the universe. Stars consist mostly of hydrogen in a plasma state. However naturally occurring hydrogen is rare on earth due to the lightness of the gas. Hydrogen however forms compounds with most elements, and is found in water and most organic compounds.

Hydrogen was discovered in 1671 by Richard Boyle when he noted the reaction between iron filings and diluted acids producing hydrogen gas.

Hydrogen is used in the study of quantum mechanics; however the two largest uses for hydrogen are in fossil fuel processing and ammonia production, mostly for the fertilizer market.

Hydrogen is also used as a coolant in some power stations but needs to be kept in liquid form. A power failure can cause the tanks to heat up and allow the hydrogen to vent, creating a huge risk of explosion and suffocation hazard around the venting tanks.

Hydrogen gas is extremely flammable and will burn in air in concentration from 4 to 75% by volume and forms explosive concentrations when mixed with chlorine from 5 to 95% by volume and will explode by heat, spark or sunlight.

Pure hydrogen and Oxygen mixtures burn and emit an ultraviolet light making it nearly invisible to the human eye. Hydrogen is used in many of the main engines of space shuttles.

In diving, hydrogen gas is mainly used in deep commercial diving. Due to its explosive nature when mixed with more than 4 to 5% Oxygen, it is limited to very deep diving and imposes complicated protocols to ensure that Oxygen is cleared from the lungs, blood stream and breathing equipment before breathing hydrogen can start.

Unlike neon, hydrogen does distort the diver's voice and a voice scrambler is needed for communication. Hydrogen-Oxygen mixes in diving are referred to as Hydrox. Hydrogen narcosis produces symptoms such as hallucinations, disorientation and confusion, which are similar to hallucinogenic drugs and is mainly experienced when exceeding 303 m (1,000 ft) on hydrogen mixtures.

Although hydrogen is less narcotic than nitrogen, it is very rarely used in diving due to the complexity of its volatile nature. From tests with divers diving to 500 m (1,650 ft) with a hydrogen–helium–Oxygen (Hydreliox) mixture that contained 49% hydrogen it was found that the neurological symptoms of high-pressure nervous syndrome were only moderate and less than if only helium and Oxygen was used making it a better choice than Tri-Mix with Oxygen/helium/nitrogen (less narcosis than Tri-Mix and less HPNS symptoms than heliox). Hydrogen's diffusion speed is around 3.7 times faster than nitrogen.

CO_2:

Atomic Number .... - (CO_2 is a compound)
Symbol on periodic table .. CO_2
Atomic weight .... 44.01 g
Melting Point .... - 109 °F
Boiling Point .... - 70 °F
Density .... 1.977 g/L in gas form

CO_2 is a naturally occurring gas found at concentrations of about 0.039% by volume in air. CO_2 is colorless and gives a sour taste (due to the gas dissolving into the mucus membrane and saliva to form a carbonic acid) if inhaled in concentrations higher than found in standard air.

Being a natural byproduct of combustion and metabolism it can be distilled from air, however this is not a very effective way and chemical routes are a better option. One such way is hydrochloric acid and calcium bicarbonate (limestone) reactions.

CO_2 was first observed in the seventeenth century by Jan Baptist van Helmont. He found that when burning charcoal in a closed container the mass of the ash was less than that of the original charcoal and concluded that the rest must have been lost in gas form.

In the 1750's Joseph Black found that when heating limestone, a dense gas can be found.

In 1772, Joseph Priestley caused the invention of soda water by publishing a paper entitled 'Impregnating Water with Fixed Air'. He described the process of producing CO_2 and forcing the gas to dissolve in water.

Today CO_2 is used in the food, oil and chemical industry.

CO_2 is used in consumer products that require pressurized gas due to its inexpensive cost and is used in many life vests, air guns, paintball guns, soda drinks, fire extinguishers, welding, blasting in coal mines and in some cases to kill pests.

In diving, CO_2 retention can be a problem and can lead to CO_2 poisoning which symptoms can range from heavy breathing, headaches, nausea to unconsciousness or blackout.

CO_2 is converted to bicarbonate to help the body maintain a normal Ph balance. About 75% of the CO_2 in the body is converted to carbonic acid (H_2CO_3) which can be converted to bicarbonate (HCO_3^-) when needed. Excess CO_2 is expelled from the body and receptors (chemoreceptors) in the arch of the aorta and throughout the arteries send signals to the respiratory center that allows it to control your breathing.

Prolonged exposure to moderate concentrations can cause acidosis as well as an adverse effect on calcium phosphorus metabolism resulting in an increase in calcium deposits in soft tissues.

CO_2 is toxic to the heart and can affect the heart's ability to contract, the higher the percentage of CO_2 in the breathing mix the more adverse the affect.

1% can cause drowsiness after prolonged exposures.
2% causes mild narcosis, increased blood pressure, higher pulse rate and reduced hearing.
5% causes difficulty breathing, dizziness, confusion, headache and shortness of breath and possible panic.
8% causes headache, sweating, dim vision, tremor and loss of consciousness after exposure of five to ten minutes.

Note that these are percentages based on partial pressures when the diver is at 1 atm and that when diving to depth a smaller percentage of CO2 will reach the same partial pressure as a larger percentage on the surface. A poorly tuned regulator can not only cause pulmonary barotrauma or edema, but also CO2 retention and a higher work of breathing that produces even more CO2.

For long dives CO2 exposure must be kept below 5mbars, normal level is around 5.2 kPa, 0.052 ATA or 39mmHg. 6.2kPa is the upper limit in the normal range, over 8.5kPa sudden incapacitation is highly likely. Experiments done on working divers found a level between 6.5 to 7.5KPa not to be uncommon. A diver (especially if unfit) working against a current can easily reach these values.

When breathing elevated partial pressures of Oxygen, higher levels of Oxygen dissolves into the blood and tissues and limits the ability of the blood to transport CO2 out of the tissues. This results in higher venous and tissue CO2 levels than would normally be found in the body. The result can be a build up of CO2 that can over time lead to CO2 poisoning.

Skip breathing, poorly tuned regulators and poor quality regulators that are hard to breathe from and hard work, will increase the amount of CO2 produced by the body. This will further complicate your dive by increasing nitrogen narcosis and the risk of getting decompression sickness, and can cause Oxygen toxicity symptoms at lower levels of PPO2 as it lowers your tolerance for O2 toxicity.

Higher than normal levels of CO_2 in the body will cause the divers breathing to increase and use up the available gas supply faster. By breathing faster the diver may over breathe a regulator and get the feeling of being starved of gas or not getting enough gas. The diver may start to panic and this in turn will increase narcosis, breathing, CO_2 production (forming a loop), susceptibility to CNS toxicity and decompression sickness. If the diver does not realize something is wrong and correct their breathing a disaster may not be far off.

CO_2 poisoning symptoms include rapid breathing, shortness of breath, headache (normally throbbing or severe), dizziness, confusion, nausea, visual problems, tremors, muscle twitching, convulsions, unconsciousness and death.

It is noted that rapid increase of CO_2 can cause blackouts without any warning and can result from working hard when swimming against a current on the surface, poor breathing habits, contaminated gas with high levels of CO_2 in or hard breathing regulators (building up CO_2) and then making a rapid descent.

Elevated levels of CO_2 cause the blood vessels to dilate and have multiple effects on the body. Dilated blood vessels will cause more inert gas to be dissolved into the tissues quicker and can pre-dispose a diver to decompression sickness.

The CO_2 can increase any bubbles already found in tissues or blood and compound matters even more. The increase of blood flow to the skin and tissues can increase heat loss. This can not only potentially lead to chilling the diver, but gas dissolves per volume into a colder tissue more than when warm (warm beer loses its bubbles as it heats up) and can result in the diver on-gassing even more inert gas and pre-dispose him/her even more to decompression sickness.

CO:

Atomic Number .... - (CO is a compound)
Symbol on periodic table .. CO
Melting Point .... - 337 °F
Boiling Point .... - 313 °F
Density .... 1.250 g/L @ 32 °F

Carbon monoxide is a colorless, odorless, tasteless gas and is slightly lighter than air; it is highly toxic to humans especially under elevated pressures. CO is a byproduct of incomplete combustion (due to not enough Oxygen to produce CO2) and is normally found in dive tanks due to poor compressor filters, faulty compressors or fumes entering the compressor intake.

From prehistoric times till today CO is used in melting of iron and other metals, and the Romans and Greeks used it as an execution gas. The gas was first described by Dr Analdus de Villa Nova in around the 11th century, and in 1776 de Lassone produced CO by heating zinc oxide and coke. In 1800 William Cumberland Cruikshank found that the gas was made up of carbon and Oxygen.

CO was possibly used by the Nazis in executions, but this was never confirmed and is only speculated today.

CO is used in packaging systems with fresh meat products such as beef, pork and fish to keep them looking fresh as the carbon monoxide combines with myoglobin in the tissue to form carboxymyoglobin, a bright cherry red pigment. This stable red color can make the meat look fresher much longer than normally packaged meat.

CO bonds about 200 to 225 times more regularly with blood cells than Oxygen and keeps clinging to the cells, blocking the body's ability to take up Oxygen and remove CO_2. The combination with hemoglobin is called carboxyhemoglobin.

CO is a colorless, odorless, tasteless and highly toxic gas and concentrations as low as 667 ppm (parts per million) may cause up to 50% of the body's hemoglobin to convert to carboxyhemoglobin that may result in seizures, coma and death.

Symptoms of CO poisoning include headache, nausea, vomiting, dizziness, fatigue, weakness, confusion, disorientation, syncope, possible seizures, retinal hemorrhages, cyanosis, possible unconsciousness and death.

CO binds to other molecules including myoglobin and mitochondrial cytochrome oxidase and CO exposure is damaging to the heart and CNS system.

Smokers constantly take in CO and one cigarette can affect the diver's gas transport ability for hours. A single cigarette can cut a diver's lung volume down to as low as 50% for an hour or more.

Chapter 2

EANx, Nitrox, Enriched Air

History

Many people still wonder what exactly nitrox is and why anyone would want to dive with anything else than air. This is not surprising since until 1991 EANx was still seen as the black gas, devil gas or voodoo gas. Many misperceptions and misunderstandings have led to fear and unwillingness in using and supporting nitrox diving. With the efforts of tech divers, nitrox slowly made its way into the recreational world and is today a common diving gas in many places. Some liveaboards do not even allow air diving any more due to the number of dives done on a liveaboard.

As it turns out, if you are breathing air at this moment then you are in fact breathing nitrox. Nitrox is nothing more than a nice name for a mixture of nitrogen and Oxygen. Since air is a mixture of both, we can call it nitrox. A mix that has 20 to 21% Oxygen is called a normoxic or normal Oxygen content mix.

Enriched air nitrox on the other hand is a mixture where the gas is enriched by adding more Oxygen to the mix or removing nitrogen so that the result is a mix that has more than 21% Oxygen in the mix. A mix that has less than 20% Oxygen is normally called hypoxic. Although some will call 18% Oxygen mixes a normoxic mix.

So why would we want to dive with a gas mix that contains more Oxygen? Good question, since raising the O2 content in the mix does not do much for the body carrying more O2 to the cells. What is important is that there is less nitrogen in the mix.

Since bottom time is related to the amount of inert gas our body uptakes then having less nitrogen in the mix will allow us more bottom time. For safety we can elect to not use the added bottom time and have a potential safer dive.

EAD

Since you are breathing less nitrox per minute for a specific depth compared to an air diver at the same depth, you can descend deeper than the air diver before you will have the same PPN2. An EAD (Equivalent air depth) value is the depth that the PPN2 in air would be the same as a diver on EANx at a specific depth.

EAD ft formula:

$$\frac{(1 - FO2) * (Depth + 33)}{0.79} - 33$$

EAD m formula:

$$\frac{(1 - FO2) * (Depth + 10)}{0.79} - 10$$

Example:

EAD for EAN32 @ 100 ft =

$$\frac{(1 - 0.32) * (100 + 33)}{0.79} - 33$$

= 81.48 ft

EAD for EAN32 @ 30 m =

$$\frac{(1 - 0.32) * (30 + 10)}{0.79} - 10$$

= 24.43 m

Breathing nitrox does not affect your breathing rate in general and your gas supply will last the same as on air.

In rare cases it has been noted that people get headaches while diving on nitrox which is linked to the increased PPO2 in the mix. Most people have a trigger to breathe when the amount of CO2 in the body reaches a certain amount or level, but there is also a low O2 trigger which is normally weak in most people. In rare cases the trigger to breathe is actually the low O2 trigger that is normally found in smokers, but not always.

Since diving on nitrox raises the PPO2 more than would be found when compared to air at the same depth, it takes longer before the O2 level drops to a trigger point to breathe. The results are CO2 retention or build up of CO2 and the level of CO2 can become so high before we breathe that it becomes mildly toxic.

Now that we know our diving range of PPO2 is between 0.2 to 1.6 ata, what is the mix we should use then for our dive to have the correct PPO2 at depth?

We normally want to keep the PPO2 in the range of below or at 1.4 PPO2 at the deepest part of our dive to be safe.

Liquid O2 used for blending.

Calculating the gas needed for a dive

Now this is where our first formula comes in.

Pressure T formula :
Pg = Fg * Pd

Where
Pg is the pressure of the gas
Fg is the fraction of the gas
Pd is the absolute pressure at depth

Let's look at an example.
We do not want to exceed a 1.4 PPO2, and we want to go to 100 fsw. 100/33 = 3.0303 of hydrostatic pressure. If using meters, then divide by 10.
Example 100 ft = roughly 30.3 m / 10 = 3.03 ata.
However, the atmosphere is an additional 1 atmosphere of pressure. Therefore, the total pressure at 100 ft is 4.0303 ata.

Now all we do is put our values into our formula.
1.4 / 4.0303 = 0.347 or 34.7% nitrox

EAN34 will be fine for this dive. Although EAN34 will result in a lower than 1.4 PPO2, using EAN35 will exceed a 1.4 PPO2.

In short
Pg = Fg * Pd
Fg = Pg / Pd
Pd = Pg / Fg

Remember to use absolute pressure, thus adding 1 when converting from depth to pressure and subtracting 1 when converting from pressure to depth.

Nitrox blending from empty

Ok so now that we know we want EAN34, how do we blend it?

First, we need to calculate how much Oxygen we need in the tank in total. For this, we need the fill pressure or service pressure of a tank.

Let's take a standard 80 cu ft aluminum tank.
Standard fill pressure is 3000 psi or 207 bar, but for consistency we will use psi for calculations. 1 bar is roughly = 14.5037738 psi.

Need O2 Formula :
FO2 * Fill pressure

0.34 * 3000 = 1020 psi O2
We need 1020 psi of O2 in total.

If we had pure nitrogen we could just fill the tank with 1020 psi of Oxygen and top it up to 3000 psi with nitrogen, although not practical. Therefore, we will be topping it up with air. The problem is that air has roughly 21% Oxygen in itself. Thus, we need to add less than 1020 psi of Oxygen. The formula to calculate the amount is as follows.

O2 to add formula
((Want Fg – Fill Fg) / Fg of nitrogen in fill mix) * fill pressure

Thus, we have ((0.34 - 0.21) / 0.79) * 3000
= (0.13 / 0.79) * 3000
= 493.67 or 494 psi O2

We need to fill our tank with 494 psi of O2 and top it up to 3000 psi with air.

Let's see if we are correct.

3000 psi tank pressure total – 494 psi O2 = 2506 psi

The 2506 psi has 21% O2 so we get an additional
(2506 * 0.21) = 526 psi O2
526 + 494 = 1020 psi O2 in total

Just the right amount we needed.

Topping up a Nitrox tank with the same ending mix

A customer did a dive on an EAN34 mix and brings the tank back with 1000 psi left in the tank. The customer wants it topped up with the same blend. We could drain the tank and start from scratch, but it would be wasting gas. So let's see how we calculate this one.

We know we need a total of 1020 psi O2 (0.34 * 3000)

Let's see how much we already have in the tank.

Left over O2 formula:
Left over pressure * FG in tank

1000 psi left in the tank * 0.34 = 340 psi O2

Thus, we have 340 psi O2 already in the tank.

Still need O2 formula:
Total O2 Needed – Left over O2 in tank

We need an additional (1020 – 340) 680 psi of O2 in the tank.

However, we have only 2000 psi of space left to get that 680 psi of O2 in. So what percentage does that 680 psi of O2 work out to on 2000 psi?

Add O2% of fill pressure formula:
O2 pressure / pressure left to fill

680 / 2000 = 34%

Not surprising as we want the same mix as is left in the tank.

So now, we just see how much O2 to add before we top it up with air. Use O2 to add formula, pg 43.

((0.34 - 0.21) / .79) * 2000
= (0.13 / 0.79) * 2000
= 329 psi O2

We add 329 psi of O2 to the 1000 psi.

The space that is left is 3000 – 1329 or 1671 psi and that contains 21% O2 so we get an additional (0.21 * 1671) = 351 psi of O2 in the mix.

The total amount of O2 is then 340 psi left over in the tank plus 329 psi O2 added plus 351 psi O2 in air top.
Or 340 + 329 + 351 = 1020 psi O2

Topping up a Nitrox mix to a different ending mix

A customer brings in a cylinder with 1000 psi of EAN34 and wants to change the mix to EAN40.

We still have (0.34 * 1000) = 340 psi O2 in the tank.
We need (0.4 * 3000) = 1200 psi O2 in total.

So we need an additional (1200 - 340) = 860 psi O2.
We need to get that 860 psi O2 into the tank with the 2000 psi space that is left.

So what percentage does that relate to? 860 / 2000 = 43%

If we had EAN43 banked we could just top the tank of to 3000 psi. But that is unlikely. So again, how much O2 do we need to add?

((0.43 - 0.21) / 0.79) * 2000
= (0.22 / 0.79) * 2000
= 556.96 or 557 psi O2

Thus, we add an additional 557 psi of O2 to the tank and top it up with air.

1000 + 557 = 1557 psi
3000 - 1557 = 1443 psi that contains 21% O2
So we get an additional (0.21 * 1443) = 303 psi O2.
In total, we have 340 + 557 + 303 or 1200 psi of O2.

Nitrox blending using continuous flow or an EANx banked to mix

Now, let's make it even more interesting. Let's say you had EAN32 on hand and not air, how much O2 would you have needed to add to be able to top the tank up with EAN32 to get EAN40?

All we do is replace the values of air in the calculation and work it out.
((0.43 - 0.32) / 0.68) * 2000
= (0.11 / 0.68) * 2000
= 323.52 or 324 psi O2

We need to add 324 psi O2 to the tank from our left over mix of 1000 psi EAN34

1000 + 324 = 1324 psi
3000 – 1324 = 1676 psi
Of the 1676 psi, 32% is O2
(0.32 * 1676) = 536 psi O2

In total we have 340 + 324 + 536 = 1200 psi O2

Nitrox blending summary
Clean Nitrox fill

Oxygen needed to add = ((want percentage - Top up O2 : percentage) / nitrogen percentage in top up mix) * fill pressure

For an EAN50 blend we need:
((0.5 - 0.21) / 0.79) * 3000
= (0.29 / 0.79) * 3000
= 1101 psi O2

Clean Nitrox fill with top up other than air

For an EAN50 blend topped up with banked EAN32 or continuous flow EAN32 we need:
((0.5 - 0.32) / 0.68) * 3000
(0.18 / 0.68) * 3000
= 794 psi O2

Topping up a blend to the same ending blend

For a left over EAN36 @ 1200 psi topped up to EAN36 @ 3000 psi

Calculate the left over O2.
(0.36 * 1200) = 432

Calculate total O2 needed.
(0.36 * 3000) = 1080

Calculate additional O2 needed.
1080 – 432 = 648 psi O2

Calculate left over fill needed.
3000 – 1200 = 1800 psi still to fill.

Calculate EAN% for fill still needed.
648 / 1800 = 0.36 or EAN36

Calculate additional O2 to add before topping up with air.
((0.36 - 0.21) / 0.79) * 1800
= (0.15 / 0.79) * 1800
= 341.77 psi of O2 (342 psi rounded)

1200 + 342 psi O2 = 1542 psi

Fill with (3000 – 1542) =1458 psi of air.
Fill air has (0.21 *1458) = 306 psi O2
432 + 342 + 306 = 1080

Topping up a blend to a different ending blend

Convert EAN50 @ 1300 psi to EAN60 @ 3000 psi

Calculate the left over O2.
(0.5 * 1300) = 650 psi O2

Calculate total O2 needed.
We want to change the blend to EAN60.
(0.6 * 3000) = 1800 psi O2

Calculate additional O2 needed.
1800 - 650 = 1150 psi O2

Calculate left over fill needed.
3000 - 1300 = 1700 psi still to fill.

Calculate EAN% for the fill still needed.
1150 / 1700 = 0.67647 or EAN67.647 keep 3 decimal places.

Calculate the additional O2 to add, before topping up with air.
((0.67647 - 0.21) / 0.79) * 1700
= (0.46647 / 0.79) * 1700
= 1003.79 psi of O2 (1004 psi rounded)

1300 + 1004 psi O2 = 2304 psi

Fill with (3000 - 2304) =696 psi of air.
The fill air has (0.21 *696) = 146 psi O2
650 + 1004 + 146 = 1800 psi O2

Nitrox fill tips

If you are topping up a cylinder, and the EAN% that is needed in the top up mix is less than the O2% in your top up mix, then you have too much O2 already in your cylinder and need to drain some down.

Nitrox practice questions

1: Blend EAN38 @ 3000 psi

2: Top up EAN28 @ 1000 psi to 3000 psi EAN28

3: Blend EAN40 using banked EAN32 to 3000 psi

4: Convert EAN40 @ 1200 psi to 3000 psi EAN32

Chapter 3

Tri-Mix blending

History

Tri-Mix came up very closely behind heliox and helair.
Due to the problem of analyzing the helium content in the early 1920's it was easier and safer to mix helair or heliox.

In 1979 Duke University in USA did tests on Tri-Mix in a way to reduce HPNS in deep dives using heliox. The concept of using a small amount of nitrogen in the mix was proved and Tri-Mix started to become an alternative deep diving gas.

In 1991 Tom Mount created the first Tri-Mix teaching standards and Billy Deans started training Tri-Mix students.

In 2001 John Bennett became the first man to use Tri-Mix on scuba to reach 1000 ft. He would later in 2004 be lost on a dive and was declared legally dead in 2006.

In 2005 Dave Shaw set a depth record for diving on a Tri-Mix CCR in a cave in 'Bushman's Hole', South Africa. On this dive he found the body of Deon Dreyer (a lost diver who succumbed to deep water blackout on December 17, 1994) at around 270 m or 890 ft in fresh water. He would later lose his life in an attempted recovery of Dreyer's body. Shaw became entangled with the guide line at the bottom and succumbed to CO2 poisoning when trying to free himself. In a twist of fate, Dreyer's body also got entangled with Shaw's body and both came to the surface where they were recovered. In the end, he did what he set out to do. His death is a sad loss and a great blow to the technical community and is dearly missed by his friend and deep diving partner Don Shirley, who also almost lost his life on the recovery dive.

END

Tri-Mix blending needs more calculations than nitrox blending, but it is not difficult if you just do it step by step.

First, we need to be able to calculate the blend that is needed. Here we will have the same first requirement as in Nitrox. We have a set PPO2 that we do not want to exceed in addition to an END (equivalent narcotic depth). An END is an air equivalent narcotic depth that we will experience at our deepest depth on our dive.

For example, to plan a dive to 330 fsw, not exceeding a 1.4 PPO2 and an END of 100 ft, we do the following calculations:
First, we get the needed O2.

O2% needed at depth formula:
Pressure at depth * FG

Pressure at depth formula:
(Depth ft / 33) + 1
(Depth m/ 10) + 1

330 ft / 33 = 10 atm hydrostatic pressure
+1 air pressure = 11 ata total
1.4 PPO2/ 11
= 0.1272

We will use 12% O2 in our mix.

Now, the interesting and much argued calculation is how to calculate END.

There are actually three main calculations around.

The first is the same as an EAD calculation. That is only nitrogen is taken into account as narcotic and the Oxygen is ignored. This however is not totally correct, as O2 is narcotic and needs to be added to the formula.

END with only N2 narcotic

We need to calculate the nitrogen PP at 100 ft and then calculate the percentage of nitrogen needed in our mix to have the same PP at our new depth.

END N2 only formula:

$$\frac{Pnd * 0.79}{Ptd}$$

Where
Pnd = Pressure at desired narcosis depth
Ptd = Pressure at target depth

100 / 33 = 3.0303
+1 = 4.0303 ata at depth
* 0.79% nitrogen
= 3.1839 ata PPN2 @ 100 ft
/ 11 (the pressure at our new depth)
= 0.289
Or not exceeding 28%

Therefore, we have 100 – 12% O2 – 28% nitrogen = 60% helium
This formula would ask for a 12/60 mix.

END with N2 and O2 narcotic

However, that is not totally correct as the 12% O2 is narcotic in itself.

To include both nitrogen and Oxygen in the narcosis formula the calculations are as follows:

END O2 + N2 only formula:
Pnd / Ptd

Take the total pressure at our planned END.
100 / 33 = 3.0303
+1 = 4.0303 ata @ 100 ft (planned END)
/ 11 ata @ 330 ft (planned target depth)
= 0.366

Or not exceeding 36% for both Oxygen and nitrogen in total. We already have 12% O2; therefore, we can only have 24% nitrogen in the mix, leaving helium to fill up the rest.

Thus, we have 100 – 36 = 64% helium.

The mix would be 12/64; this does not sound like much of a change (4% helium), but let's put our first mix into this formula.

If you take the old mix of 12/60, you have a combination of O2 and nitrogen at 40%.

At 330 ft, it would be a PP of 0.4 * 11 = 4.4 ata.
Subtracting 1 for the atmosphere leaves us with 3.4 ata * 33 = 112.2 ft narcosis, 12 ft deeper than we wanted.

END with N2, O2 and He Narcotic

However, helium is 0.235 times as narcotic as nitrogen, but due to it being such a small amount, it is not normally used in the calculations for END. This is due to the helium only adding to narcosis when the PPHe exceeds 4.25 ata.

Let's see how the helium affects narcosis in our example.

Helium narcosis ft formula:
Narcosis for He = (0.235 * He% * total ata * 33) - 33

Helium narcosis m formula:
Narcosis for He = (0.235 * He% * total ata * 10) - 10

((0.235 * 0.64 * 11) * 33) – 33
(1.6544 * 33) – 33
= 21.59 ft

The 12/64 would actually have an END of 122 ft and not 100 ft.

If we take the original mix of 12/60 we get the following narcosis. We already saw that the Oxygen and nitrogen gave us a 112.2 ft narcosis, now let's include the He.

((0.235 * 0.60 * 11) * 33) – 33
(1.551 * 33) -33
= 18.18 ft

Adding all together we get 18.18 + 112.2 or 130.4 ft END.
Far greater than the 100 ft we wanted.

To reach the blend we want, we have to do a bit of repetitive calculations. Starting with the blend we arrived at using the oxygen and nitrogen as narcotic, 12/64, we then add one percent helium to the mix and subtract one percent nitrogen from the mix. Using the new values we recalculate and continue to add helium and subtract nitrogen until we arrive at the desired END depth we want. Alternatively, we can just use a blender program, that's why I wrote 'Gas Blender Program', easy to use excel spreadsheet to do the calculations for you.
www.antonswanepoelbooks.com/gas_blender_program.php

Blending Tri-Mix new

For a dive to 330 ft with an END that includes O2, He and nitrogen as narcotic, and PPO2 below 1.4 we need a 12/71 mix.

To blend this mix we first need to calculate the amount of He and O2 needed in the mix.

Helium need formula
FHe * fill pressure

Taking a 3000 fill pressure, we have:
0.71 * 3000 = 2130 psi He
0.12 * 3000 = 360 psi O2

We first add 2130 psi of Helium to our empty cylinder. Note, Helium does not behave like an ideal gas and thus needs to be filled slowly, or the cylinder needs to be allowed to cool and the pressure rechecked. The faster the fill is done, the more inaccurate the mix will be.

Once we added our Helium we have 3000 - 2130 = 870 psi left to fill. Of that, we need 360 psi O2. Now the calculation is basically the same as a Nitrox blend. We calculate what percentage that 360 psi is of 870 psi.
360 / 870 = 0.41379 or 41.137%

Now we just add the values to our Nitrox formula.
((0.41379 - 0.21) / 0.79) * 870
= 224.43 psi O2 needed. (224 psi rounded)

That leaves us with 646 psi to top up with air, which contains 21% O2. The O2 in this would be:
0.21 * 646 = 135.66 psi O2
135.66 psi O2 + 224 psi O2 already added = 359.66 psi O2. Easy.

Topping up a Tri-Mix blend to the same ending mix

A diver returns with 1000 psi of 12/71 and wants it topped up to 3000 psi. We could drain the tanks and start from scratch, but since helium is expensive we will top it up.

We already saw from the first calculations that we need 2130 psi of Helium and 420 psi O2 in total.

Have
0.71 * 1000 = 710 psi He
0.12 * 1000 = 120 psi O2

Still Need
2130 - 710 = 1420 psi He
360 - 120 = 240 psi O2

Add 1420 psi He to the tank.
We now have 1000 + 1420 = 2420 psi total.
3000 - 2420 = 580 psi left to top up

However, we still need 240 psi of O2 in that space.
240 / 580 = 0.41379 or EAN41.379 needed.
Using the Nitrox formula, we have:
((0.41379 - 0.21) / 0.79) * 580 = 149.62 psi O2 (150 psi rounded)

Add 150 psi O2 to the tank.
2420 + 150 psi O2 = 2570 psi

We need to now add 3000 - 2570 = 430 psi of air, that contains 0.21 * 430 = 90.3 psi O2

Adding all together: original 120 psi O2 left + the 150 psi O2 we added + 90.3 psi in the air = 360.3 psi O2. Just what we needed.

Converting a Nitrox mix to a Tri-Mix mix

Now let's say we dove to 150 ft using EAN28 and we want to go to 220 ft the next day.

If we still have 1200 psi of EAN28 left in our tank and we wanted 18/35 for the next dive, how do we convert it to Tri-Mix?

Need
0.35 * 3000 = 1050 psi He
0.18 * 3000 = 540 psi O2

Have
0.28 * 1200 = 336 psi O2

Ok, now we just add the needed Helium to our tank, leaving us with 1200 psi + 1050 = 2250 psi.

We know we still need 540 - 336 = 204 psi O2.
We have 3000 - 2250 = 750 psi left to get it into the tank.

204 / 750 = 0.272

Back to our Nitrox formula
((0.272 - .021) / 0.79 * 750 = 58.86 psi O2 (59 psi rounded).
We add our 59 psi O2 to our tank and get 2250 + 59 = 2309 psi

The rest is 3000 - 2309 = 691 psi we top up with air, that contains 0.21 * 691 = 145 psi O2.

In total, we have 336 + 59 + 145 = 540 psi O2
Spot on.

Topping up a Tri-Mix to a different ending mix

After our 220 ft dive we come back with 800 psi of 18/35 in our tanks. We want to do a dive to 330 ft and will use the 12/71 mix.

Need
0.71 * 3000 = 2130 psi He
0.12 * 3000 = 360 psi O2

Have
0.35 * 800 = 280 psi He
0.18 * 800 = 144 psi O2

Still need
2130 - 280 = 1850 psi He
360 - 144 = 216 psi O2

Now it is simple, we add the needed Helium to our tank, leaving us with 800 + 1850 = 2650 psi in the tank. We have then 3000 - 2650 = 350 psi left to get our 216 psi O2 in.

216 / 350 = 0.61714 or 61.714%
((0.61714 - 0.21) / 0.79) * 350 = 180.379 psi O2

Add 180 psi O2 to the tank = 2650 + 180 = 2830 psi

We still need 3000 - 2830 = 170 psi of air that has 0.21 * 170 = 35.7 or 36 psi O2

In total, we have 144 + 180 + 36 = 360 psi O2

Mixing with continuous flow EANx or Banked EANx

Now, if we only had banked or continuous flow EANx and want to blend Tri-Mix we have to do just a bit of recalculation, but not much.

Let's take a blend of 20/40 and use EAN32 to mix with.

Need
0.4 * 3000 = 1200 He
0.2 * 3000 = 600 psi O2

Add 1200 Helium to the tank = 3000 – 1200 = 1800 psi left.

In that, we need to get our 600 psi O2.
600 / 1800 = 0.33333 or 33.33%
((0.33333 - 0.32) / 0.68) * 1800
= 35.29 psi O2 needed

Add 35 psi O2 to our tank
1200 + 35 = 1235 psi total
The rest 3000 – 1235 = 1765 psi will be EAN32

Therefore, we get 0.32 * 1765 = 564.8 or 565 psi O2
In total, we now have 35 + 565 = 600 psi O2

Mixing with impure Helium

In some parts of the world it is difficult to locate pure helium. Since it can be fatal if one breathes pure helium, a bit of O2 is added to the helium, normally in the range of 2 to 20% O2. This causes a problem when trying to blend, however nothing that cannot be handled with a bit of calculation.

Taking a blend of 18/40 and assuming our helium has only 98% Helium and 2% O2.

Need
0.4 * 3000 = 1200 psi of He
0.18 * 3000 = 540 psi of O2

Ok, since our Helium is only 98% pure we need
1200 / 0.98 = 1224.489 psi He, or 1225 psi He

From that 1225 psi, we get 2% O2, so we now have
0.02 * 1225 = 24.5 psi (25 psi rounded) of O2 in the tank

Still need 540 - 25 = 515 psi of O2.

Add 1225 psi Helium to our empty tank.

3000 - 1225 = 1775 is left.
515 / 1775 = 0.2901408 or 29.01%
((0.2901408 - 0.21) / 0.79) * 1775 = 180 psi O2 needed
Add 180 psi O2 to the tank = 1225 + 180 = 1405 psi total

So we need 3000 - 1405 = 1595 psi of air, that has
0.21 * 1595 = 334.95 psi O2
In total, we have 25 + 180 + 335 = 540 psi O2.

Topping up or changing a left over blend while using impure Helium

If you mix while using impure helium or industrial helium, then you need to subtract the have helium amount from the want helium amount before you divide by the percentage of helium.

Example
Have 1000 psi of 20/35 and wish to mix 20/40 @ 3000 psi using helium 2/98 (2% Oxygen in helium mix)

Have
0.2 * 1000 = 200 psi O2
0.35 * 1000 = 350 psi He

Want
0.2 * 3000 = 600 psi O2
0.4 * 3000 = 1200 psi He

Still need
600 - 200 = 400 psi O2
1200 - 350 - 850 psi He

Fill amounts
He = 850 / 0.98 = 867.35 psi He
This is the actual amount of Helium to be added to the cylinder. Of that amount of Helium added we have the following amount of Oxygen in it.
867.35 * 0.02 = 17.35 psi O2

So now, we only need the following amount of Oxygen still to be added to the cylinder.
400 - 17.35 = 382.65 Total O2 needed

The amount of Oxygen needs to be added in the following space.
3000 – (1000 + 867.35) = 1132.65

Thus, the Oxygen percent will need to be
382.65 / 1132.65 = 0.337836

If we top up with air, we need to first put the following amount of pure Oxygen in the cylinder before topping up with air.
((0.337836 – 0.21) / 0.79) * 1132.65
= 183 psi O2

For interest: If we were to have topped up the mix with EAN32 we would have only needed to add the following amount of Oxygen to the mix before topping up with EAN32
((0.337836 – 0.32) / 0.68) * 1132.65
= 29.71 psi O2

Tri-Mix summary

Blending Tri-Mix new

Blend 12/71

Need
0.71 * 3000 = 2130 psi He
0.12 * 3000 = 360 psi O2

3000 – 2130 = 870 psi
= 360 / 870 = 0.41379
((0.41379 - 0.21) / 0.79) * 870
= 224.43 psi O2 needed

Add 2130 psi He, add 224.43 psi O2, top up with air to 3000 psi

Topping up a Tri-Mix blend to the same ending mix

Top up 1000 psi of 12/71

Need
0.71 * 3000 = 2130 psi He
0.12 * 3000 = 360 psi O2

Have
0.71 * 1000 = 710 psi He
0.12 * 1000 = 120 psi O2

Still Need
2130 - 710 = 1420 psi He
360 - 120 = 240 psi O2

3000 - 2420 = 580 psi left
240 / 580 = 0.41379
((0.41379 - 0.21) / 0.79) * 580 = 149.6

Add 1420 psi He
Add 150 psi O2
Top to 3000 with air

Converting a Nitrox mix to a Tri-Mix mix

Convert EAN28 @ 1200 psi to 18/35

Need
0.35 * 3000 = 1050 psi He
0.18 * 3000 = 540 psi O2

Have
0.28 * 1200 = 336 psi O2

Still need
540 – 336 = 204 psi O2

Add 1050 psi He to the tank.
1200 + 1050 psi He = 2250 psi
We have 3000 – 2250 = 750 psi left to get it into the tank.
204 / 750 = 0.272

Back to our Nitrox formula
((0.272 - 0.21) / 0.79 * 750 = 58.86 psi O2 (59 psi rounded).

Add 59 psi O2 to tank.
2250 + 59 psi O2 = 2309 psi total
Top to 3000 with air.

Topping up a Tri-Mix to a different ending mix

Convert 1000 psi 10/50 to 12/60 @ 3000 psi

Need
0.60 * 3000 = 1800 psi He
0.12 * 3000 = 360 psi O2

Have
0.50 * 1000 = 500 psi He
0.10 * 1000 = 100 psi O2

Still need
1800 – 500 = 1300 psi He
360 – 100 = 260 psi O2

1000 + 1300 = 2300 psi
3000 – 2300 = 700 psi
260 / 700 = 0.3714
((0.3714 - 0.21) / 0.79) * 700 = 143 psi O2

Add 1300 psi he to 2300 psi, add 143 psi O2 to 2443, top up with air to 3000 psi

Mixing with continuous flow EANx or Banked EANx

Blend of 18/45 and use EAN28 to mix with

Need
0.45 * 3000 = 1350 He
0.18 * 3000 = 540 psi O2

3000 – 1350 = 1650
540 / 1650 = 0.32727
((0.32727 - 0.28) / 0.72) * 1650
= 108 psi O2

Add 1350 psi He
Add 108 psi O2
Top up to 3000 with EAN28

Mixing with impure Helium

Blend 12/71 with helium 2/98

Need
0.71 * 3000 = 2130 He
0.12 * 3000 = 360 O2

Total he = 2130 / 0.98 = 2173.46 psi He (2173 psi rounded)
O2 from He = 2173 * 0.02 = 43.46 or 43 psi O2
Need 360 – 43 = 317 psi O2

3000 – 2173 = 827 psi
317 / 827 = 0.3833
((0.3833 - 0.21) / 0.79) * 827
= 181 psi O2

Add 2173 psi He, add 181 psi O2, top up with air to 3000

Tri-Mix blending tips

Remember that the faster you fill, the warmer your cylinder will become, and the further your mix will be out. In addition, if you drain a cylinder down, let it drain slowly down to minimize the cooling of the cylinder.

If you are draining multiple cylinders down and the starting pressures are different, or the speed that you drain them down is different, then the ending temperatures of the cylinders will be different. This will result in the mixtures in the cylinders to not be the same even if you added the same amount of gas to them, unless you allow them to settle and reach the same temperature before filling.

Remember as temperature goes up, so does the pressure. Therefore, the pressure you see on the gauge will not be the pressure that will be in the cylinder once it cools down. You might in many cases need to fill the cylinder to a higher pressure than wanted so that when it cools down it will be at the desired pressure.

If possible, fill to the desired pressure when the cylinder is hot or just short of the desired pressure if filling slowly and the cylinders are cool, then shake the cylinders or tip them upside down a few times to allow the mixes to settle faster.

Analyze the mix and see how far it is out. From here, you will be able to judge how much you still need to top up to, to get your desired mix.

After time you will get to know your blending system and will also know by feel how much you need to over fill the cylinder when hot so as to have the correct mix when it cools down.

Another problem with Tri-Mix blending is that the formula often calls for small amounts of gas to be added. However, pressure gauges are often marked in 20 psi or higher increments and this coupled with inaccurate pressure gauges can make blending a problem, for instance when trying to add 33 psi on a gauge with 20 psi increments.

When filling you may want to close the cylinders and bleed the fill line on every gas change, as this will ensure you do not add more of a gas than wanted.

First pressurize the fill line with the new gas before opening the cylinders. This will ensure the gas in the cylinders does not flow back into the fill line.

With practice, you can fill multiple mixes at the same time; this however calls for fast reactions and a cool head, as you need to know when to close what cylinder at what pressure. Also, do not open a higher filled cylinder before the lower filled one reaches the same pressure when changing gas. For instance if you fill two cylinders and the first one calls for 500 psi O2 and the second 1000 psi O2, you would shut the first cylinder off at 500 psi and continue filling the second to 1000 psi. Then after bleeding the lines and pressurizing them with air, you would open the first cylinder that has 500 psi O2 in and fill that to 1000 psi before opening the second cylinder.

Do not exceed the second cylinder's pressure of 1000 psi and then open the second cylinder, as that will cause the gas from the first cylinder to flow into the second cylinder, ruining both mixes.

Tri-Mix practice questions

1: Mix 13/65 @ 3000 psi

2: Top up 18/45 @ 1200 psi to 18/45 @ 3000 psi

3: Convert 20/35 @ 800 psi to 17/42 @ 3000 psi

4: Mix 20/35 using banked EAN28 as fill instead of air

5: Mix 19/40 with helium containing 2% Oxygen

Chapter 4

Helair

History

Outside military and science use, helair was mostly used in tech divers doing deep cave and wreck dives. Due to its ease of blending and analyzing, helair became popular when helium analyzers were scarce. Nowadays it is popular mostly due to its lower cost than Tri-Mix.

Helair is a hypoxic Tri-Mix, blended without using Oxygen by blending helium and air to create a Tri-Mix mixture. However, the O2 content cannot be greater than 21% unless you use banked or continuous flow EANx to blend with helium, but this is strictly speaking not helair anymore and would more be heleanx.

Helair blending is handy when you either need a quick fill, O2 is not available, O2 compatibility is a problem, or if Tri-Mix blending is too expensive. However, you need to be flexible in your dive planning as helair blending limits the mixes you can create. Adjusting your dive to a helair mix is easier when using rebreathers.

Helair is very easy to blend and you do not need O2 cleaned equipment in blending or using helair, this makes it a very cheap alternative to Tri-Mix blending.

With helair blending, you have to choose what is more important for you, the O2 content, or the helium content. Once you have decided which is more important, you just work out how much helium to add to the cylinder and top up with air.

Helair blends follow a sliding scale with the helium going up roughly 5% for every 1% drop in Oxygen from 21%. Although we call blends to the nearest percentage, the actual blend is always a bit off.

For instance, a 10/50 will be in the range of 10.5/50 to 10/53 depending on the amount of air you add. If you drop the Oxygen content to 8%, you will gain roughly 10% helium, making an 8.4/60 blend.

Mixing Helair from empty

Mixing with Helium as priority

Let's say we want 50% helium in our mix.

Need
0.5 * 3000 = 1500 psi He

Add 1500 psi He to the empty tank.
The left over pressure is 3000 – 1500 = 1500 psi

Top up to 3000 psi with air.
The 1500 psi air used in the top up contains
0.21 * 1500 = 315 psi O2

That would be
315 / 3000 = 10.5%
Therefore, our mix would be 10.5/50 (commonly called 10/50)

Mixing with Oxygen as priority

What if you wanted 14% O2, how much helium do you need to add?

First, calculate what psi O2 would create 14%
0.14 (% desired) * 3000 (service rating of cylinder) = 420 psi O2

How much air would we need to get 420 psi O2?

Since air has 21% O2, we need
420 / 0.21 = 2000 psi of air to get 420 psi O2

The left over pressure is 3000 – 2000 = 1000 psi that is filled with helium.

1000 psi He / 3000 psi tank fill = 33.3%

Thus, our mix would be 14/33

Topping up an existing Helair mix

If we had 1500 psi of 10.5/50 and wanted to top it off to 3000 psi.

Need
0.5 * 3000 = 1500 psi

Have
0.5 * 1500 = 750 psi

Still need
1500 - 750 = 750 psi He

Add 750 psi helium to cylinder to 2250 psi, and then fill to 3000 psi with air.

Changing a Helair mix to a different Helair mix

You can change Helair blends easily; just use the helium as priority.

If you have a left over mix 10.5/50 @ 1000 psi and want 8.4/60 @ 3000 psi you get the following calculations:

Need
0.6 * 3000 = 1800 psi He

Have
0.5 * 1000 = 500 psi He

Still need
1800 – 500 = 1300 psi He

Add 1300 psi helium to left over blend until 2300 psi, and then fill to 3000 psi with air.

Blending Helair with impure Helium

Ok, just to make things interesting. What if you had impure helium, how would that affect your mix?

Let's use our helium as priority and go for 50% while using helium that has 2% O2 in it.

Need
0.5 * 3000 = 1500 psi He
1500 psi He / 0.98 = 1531 psi He needed to make 50%

Of that 1531 * 0.02 = 30.62 psi O2

3000 - 1531 = 1469 of air
1469 * 0.21 = 308.49 psi O2
308.49 + 30.62 = 339.11 psi O2 in total
339.11 / 3000 = 0.113 or 11.3%

Our ending mix would be 11/50

Helium and EANx blending

A drawback when using helair, is that the Oxygen content cannot be greater than 21%, however if you have banked or continuous flow EANx, you can do some creative blending. You can still blend with either the helium or Oxygen as priority. This mix is normally called Helitrox or Hyperoxic Tri-Mix.

Blending with Helium as priority

Say you have EAN32 and want to use it to create a blend with 40% helium, what would the ending blend be?

0.4 * 3000 = 1200 psi helium
Left over space for EAN32 = 3000 - 1200 = 1800 psi

Oxygen in the 1800 psi EAN32
0.32 * 1800 = 576 psi O2
Percentage that the Oxygen would be in the end result:
(576 / 3000) * 100 = 19.2% or 19/40
A good 200 ft mix.

Blending with Oxygen as priority

If you wanted your Oxygen to be 16%, what helium percent can you get? First, we need to calculate how much EAN32 would make 16%.

(16 / 32) * 3000 = 1500 psi.
Adding 1500 psi EAN32 to the cylinder we would have
0.32 * 1500 = 480 psi O2

Double check (480 / 3000) * 100 = 16%
3000 - 1500 = 1500 psi for the helium.
Add 1500 psi helium and top up with EAN32
1500 psi helium / 3000 = 0.5 or 50%

Our mix would be 16/50 good for 240 to 255 ft @ 1.4 PPO2.

Helium with EANx and impure Helium

Ok, just to make things even more interesting.

Say you had EAN32 banked and wanted to blend with it while using only helium, but it is industrial helium with 2% Oxygen, what now?

This is basically the same as the previous examples and you need to decide whether the helium or Oxygen is the priority.

Blending with Helium as priority

Taking banked EAN32 as the first example, we want to create a blend with 40% helium.

0.4 * 3000 = 1200 psi helium

In total we need 1200 / 0.98 = 1224.489 psi He (1225 psi rounded)

Left over space for EAN32 = 3000 - 1225 = 1775 psi

Oxygen in the 1775 psi EAN32
0.32 * 1775 = 568 psi O2

Oxygen in the helium added
1225 * 0.02 = 24.5 psi O2

Total O2 = 568 + 24.5 = 592.5 psi O2
(592.5 / 3000) * 100 = 19.75%
The mix would be 20/40, a good 200 ft mix.

Helair summary

1: Mix 12/43 Helair

0.12 * 3000 = 360 psi O2
360 / 0.21 = 1714 psi air
3000 - 1714 = 1285 psi He

Top 8.4/60 @ 1000 psi up to 3200 psi
0.6 * 3200 = 1920 psi He needed
0.6 * 1000 = 600 psi He left

Need an additional 1920 - 600 = 1320 psi helium.

Fill to 2320 psi with helium, and then top up with air to 3200 psi.

2: Change 8.4/60 @ 1200 psi to 6.3/70 @ 3200 psi

Need
0.7 * 3200 psi = 2240 psi He

Have
0.6 * 1200 psi = 720 psi He

Need an additional 2240 - 720 = 1520 psi He.

Fill to 2720 psi with helium, and then top to 3200 with air.

3: Using EAN28

Want 55% helium @ 3000 psi.

0.55 * 3000 = 1650 psi He
Add 1650 psi He to the cylinder and top up with EAN28
3000 - 1650 = 1350 psi left over for EAN28

0.28 * 1350 = 378 psi O2
(378 / 3000) * 1000 = 12.6%
The mix would be 12.6/55

4: Want 15% Oxygen
(15 / 28) 3000 = 1607 psi of EAN28
3000 - 1607 = 1393 psi of helium
(1393 / 3000) * 100 = 46.4% helium
The resulting mix is 15/46

Helair practice questions

1: Fill 10/50 @ 3000 psi

2: How much air do you need to have a 15% O2 mix and what would the He% be? (3000 psi)

Chapter 5

Heliox

History

Heliox is another interesting mix. Here we take pure Oxygen and helium to create a mixture that has no nitrogen in the mix. Heliox has been in use since the 1930s.

Oxygen is widely used in medical treatments, especially when there is upper airway construction. This is due to the low density of the gas. The gas is easy to mix and easy to analyze, especially if you do not have a helium analyzer.

Heliox is used in deep diving, but there is a problem in using the gas for very deep dives. Since there is no nitrogen in the mix, symptoms of HPNS will occur shallower than would have occurred on a Tri-Mix mixture.

The thought is that the pressure experienced on deep dives compresses the lipid cells so much that it can disrupt brain signals, causing problems for the diver. By having a small percentage of nitrogen in the mix, the nitrogen will have a counter effect and make the lipid cells swell out a bit to counter for the extreme pressure. Normally between 5 and 10% nitrogen is enough. However, HPNS is normally only a problem when diving deeper than 500 ft or 150 m on Heliox.

Blending Heliox

Like helair, you basically need to decide whether the O2 or the helium content is more important, and see what is left.

Make a heliox mix for 280 ft with PPO2 not exceeding 1.4 PPO2
280 / 33 = 8.484 + 1 = 9.484
1.4 / 9.484 = 14.7% O2 we could go for 14.7% or just use 14%

For a 14% O2 we would have 100 - 14 = 86% left
Our mix would be 14/86
Now you can use either O2 or helium to calculate the psi needed. Let's do both.
0.86 * 3000 = 2580 psi He
0.14 * 3000 = 420 psi O2

You would add either 420 psi O2 first and top up with helium or you can start with the helium first and then add the O2 later.

Heliox and impure Helium

So, we want to create a Heliox mix with 60% helium, however the helium contains 2% Oxygen. How do we blend this mix?

Need
0.6 * 3000 = 1800 psi He

Actual Helium needed formula:
He pressure needed * FHe in tank

Where FHe = fraction of helium in tank.

1800 / 0.98 = 1837 psi He (actual He needed)

Left over pressure is 3000 - 1837 = 1163 psi

O2 in He tank formula:
FO2 * He fill pressure

Where FO2 = fraction of Oxygen in tank.

O2 in helium is 0.02 * 1837 = 36.74
Total O2 = 1163 + 36.74 = 1199.74
1199.74 / 3000 = 0.39991 or 40% O2

Heliox summary

1: Blend 25/75 Heliox

0.75 * 3000 = 2250 psi He
0.25 * 3000 = 750 psi O2

Heliox practice questions

1: Blend 18/82 Heliox

2: Blend 40/60 Heliox

Chapter 6

What if ...

... you top up an existing mix with air or any other gas?

Let's say we have a cylinder with 1000 psi of EAN28, what would happen to it if we topped it off with air?

Have
1000 psi * 0.28 = 280 psi O2

Now we calculate what we get from the fill.
3000 psi - 1000 psi = 2000 psi
This has 2000 psi * 0.21 = 420 psi O2.

In total we will have 280 psi + 420 psi = 700 psi O2.
This 700 psi O2 is in a cylinder with a 3000 psi service rating.
The percentage this 700 psi represents is 700 / 3000 = 0.2333 or 23% O2 in the mix.

For a 20/35 of 1000 psi when topped off with air, we have:
0.35 * 1000 psi = 350 psi He
0.20 * 1000 psi = 200 psi O2

O2 from top up is:
0.21 * 2000 psi = 420 psi O2

Total O2 is
200 + 420 = 620 psi O2

620 / 3000 = 0.2067 or 20.67% O2
350 / 3000 = 0.1166 or 11.66% He

The ending mix would be 20/11.66 or 20/12

You can mix together anything you want to create a new mix. All you need to do is calculate the amount of Oxygen and helium in both the left over mix and the gas that will be added to the cylinder when topping up.

This is where you can be creative and use left over helium or Oxygen to create a new mix. Many boosters struggle to boost when the input pressure falls to below 500 psi.

500 psi on a 3000 psi rated cylinder would give you 16.66% Helium in your mix if you topped it off with air or EANx. But if you leave 600 psi in the tank and then top it off, you will get 20% Helium.

If you top it off with EAN28 you would get a 22.4/20 mix, good for a 160 ft dive.

With pre planning you can make many mixes from left over gas that would otherwise have been drained and lost.

Chapter 7

Rebreather calculations

When blending for CCR rebreathers, you normally use 1 PPO2 at depth for calculating the diluent mix.

This allows you to easily flush the unit down at depth should you get an O2 spike. The unit keeps the PPO2 at a constant preset value (normally 1.3 PPO2), this causes the fraction of O2 to change with depth. However, this raises the question of what are you actually breathing if your FO2 changes.

For example, how does a 1.3 PPO2 affect the rest of the mix at depth? Let's have a look.

So, we want to go to 330 ft and would like our PPO2 not to exceed a value of 1. We also want an END of around 110 ft. A 9/67 mix would do nicely (calculating He as narcotic).

First we need to calculate what the actual O2% is.
330 / 33 = 10 + 1 = 11 ata (pressure at depth)
1.3 PPO2 / 11 ata = 11.82% O2 in breathing loop

Now we calculate what percentage the rest of the gas makes up.
100 - 11.82 = 88.18% for the rest of the gas

The rest of the gas is still in a ratio of 67% He and 24% Nitrogen
Therefore, we have

New Helium percentage formula:
((loop% - O2%) * original He%)
(original He% + original Nitrogen%)

Actual He = (88.18 * 67) / (67 + 24)
= (5908.06) / (91)
= 64.9%

New N2 percentage formula:
100 – (New O2% + New He%)

Actual Nitrogen would be
100 - (11.82 + 64.9) = 23.28%
Actual loop mix is now 11.82/64.9 not 9/67

Nitrogen and O2 narcosis = (((1 - 0.649) * 11) * 33) - 33
= 94.413 ft

Helium narcosis = ((0.235 * 0.649) * 11) * 33) – 33
= 22.36 ft

Total narcosis = 116.7 ft
This new mix would give us a 116.7 ft END not 110 ft as planned.

Bailout mix

This mix of 11.82/64.9 or 12/65 can now be used as a bailout mix. This will ensure that when you bailout there is no O2, helium or nitrogen spike. This smooth bailout makes it easier on your body, keeps the narcosis the same, and helps to prevent ICD.

The same calculations can be used in determining what the loop gas would be at any depth, allowing the diver to select the best bailout gas for any depth while making sure that the bailout mix is close to or the same as what is in the rebreather loop.

Doing this makes it safer for the diver and helps to prevent ICD DCS.

Rebreather summary

Actual Helium Formula

$$\frac{((100\% - O2\%) * \text{original He}\%)}{(\text{original He}\% + \text{original N2}\%)}$$

Actual Nitrogen = 100 – (O2% + New He%)

Rebreather loop practice questions

What is in the loop of a mix of 8/60 with 1.3 PPO2 at 330 ft? In addition, what is the END?

Chapter 8

Blending with ICD DCS in mind

What is ICD DCS?

One of the problems with deep diving is the possible need for gas changes underwater. For OC you need to change gasses in order to speed up your decompression time, for a rebreather you may need to bailout.

A problem can occur if the mix you are switching to contains too little helium.

A common practice in the 1980's to early 2000 was to switch from a gas containing a high percentage of inert gas, normally helium, to either air or a Nitrox blend with no helium in the mix. The thought was to get off the helium as quickly as possible. It was assumed that inert gas does not on- and off-gas separately and that the sum of the partial pressures of the gas must make up the whole of the ambient pressure.

Thus, it was thought that if one was saturated with one gas, another gas cannot diffuse into the tissues until the first one off-gassed completely. Tests done in 1975 by Lambertsen and Iicula found that different gasses diffuse into the tissues independently of the other gasses around them and have little or no affect on each other.

Now it is becoming more common practice to switch to a lighter Tri-Mix blend.

Blending for ICD DSC

The current thought is that you should not let the nitrogen percent go up more than 1% for every 5% helium drop, with O2 taking up the rest of the 4%, or ideally have the O2 take up the full helium drop.

In addition, you do not want to make too big a drop in helium.

Another point is that it is ideal to not switch gas on or just before a deep stop. Rather, do the deep stops then switch, or recalculate your switch point to be further away from a deep stop. This will minimize the chance of an ICD DCS hit.

Let's say you did a dive to 330 ft (100 m) with 12/65 on OC and you want to switch at 220 ft. You will be switching to 20% O2. That is an increase of 8% O2. Thus, we can allow the nitrogen to go up 2%.

Your mix would now be 20/55.

Now you want to switch at 98 ft, a 40% O2 will do. Since you upped the O2 by 20%, you can allow the nitrogen to go up 5%.

The mix would now be 40/30.

Depending on your Deco needs you can then change to an EAN80 at 33 ft.

This would be a much smoother change than switching to air at 220 ft and then to an EAN32 and later EAN80 as was done before.

The reason for this is, if you allow the nitrogen percentage to go up, the PPN2 in your body goes up, but you are not going deeper. That means that the PPN2 tension between what is in your tissues and the surrounding pressure increases. This could increase to a point that it can cause DCS at depth.

Let's look at the previous example of what would have happened to the nitrogen and helium if we did switch to air at 220 ft.

For the blend 12/65, we have 7.666 ata at 220 ft.
0.65 * 7.666 = 4.9829 ATM for helium
0.23 * 7.666 = 1.7631 ATM for nitrogen

Switching to air, we have 0 ATM for helium, as far as the helium is concerned, you made a direct ascent from 220 ft in the time it took you to take that first breath of air. In addition, as we all know, helium's density being a lot less than nitrogen, it is a far less forgiving gas when it comes to depth changes. You get decompression sickness easier on helium than on nitrogen and normally worse as well.

The nitrogen on the other hand increases to:
0.79 * 7.666 = 6.05614 ATM Nitrogen
6.05614 / 1.7631 = 3.434 times the original PPN2 that you had in the mix. As far as narcosis goes, someone just switched your lights off.

Chapter 9

Practice answers

Answers for chapter 2

1: Blend EAN38 @ 3000 psi

Need
0.38 * 3000 = 1140 psi O2

((0.38 - 0.21) / 0.79) * 3000
=645.56 psi O2

Add 646 psi O2 and fill with air to 3000 psi

2: Top up EAN28 @ 1000 psi to 3000 psi EAN28

Want
0.28 * 3000 = 840 psi O2

Have
0.28 * 1000 = 280 psi O2

Need
840 – 280 – 560 psi O2

560 / 2000 = 0.28
((0.28 - 0.21) / 0.79) * 2000
=177 psi O2

Add 177 psi O2 to 1177 psi and fill to 3000 psi with air

3: Blend EAN40 using banked EAN32 to 3000 psi

Want
0.4 * 3000 = 1200 psi O2
((0.4 - 0.32) / 0.68) * 3000
=352.9 psi O2

Add 353 psi O2 and fill to 3000 psi with EAN32

4: Convert EAN40 @ 1200 psi to 3000 psi EAN32

Want
0.32 * 3000 = 960 psi O2

Have
0.4 * 1200 psi = 480

Need
960 – 480 = 480 psi

480 / 1800 = 0.26666
((0.26666 - 0.21) / 0.79) * 1800
= 129 psi O2

Add 129 psi O2 to 1329 psi then fill to 3000 psi with air

Answers for chapter 3

1: Mix 13/65 @ 3000 psi

Want
0.65 * 3000 = 1950 psi He
0.13 * 3000 = 390 psi O2

Need
3000 – 1950 – 1050
390 / 1050 = 0.37142
((0.37142 – 0.21) / 0.79) * 1050 = 214.5 psi

Add 1950 psi He, add 215 psi O2, fill to 3000 psi with air

2: Top up 18/45 @ 1200 psi to 18/45 @ 3000 psi

Want
0.45 * 3000 = 1350 psi he
0.18 * 3000 = 540 psi O2

Have
0.45 * 1200 = 540 psi He
0.18 * 1200 = 216 psi O2

Need
1350 – 540 = 810 psi He
540 – 216 = 324 psi O2

Add 810 psi He to mix to pressure 2010

3000 – 2010 = 990
324 / 990 = 0.3272
((0.3272 - 0.21) / 0.79) * 990 = 146.96
Add 147 psi O2; fill to 3000 psi with air

3: Convert 20/35 @ 800 psi to 17/42 @ 3000 psi

Want
0.42 * 3000 = 1260 psi He
0.17 * 3000 = 510 psi O2

Have
0.35 * 800 = 280 psi He
0.20 * 800 = 160 psi O2

Need
1260 - 280 = 980 psi He
510 - 160 = 350 psi O2

Add 980 psi He to mix to pressure 1780

3000 - 1780 = 1220
350 / 1220 = 0.28688
((0.28688 - 0.21) / 0.79) * 1220 = 118.73 psi O2

Add 119 psi O2 and fill to 3000 psi with air

4: Mix 20/35 using banked EAN28 as fill instead of air

Want
0.35 * 3000 = 1050 psi He
0.20 * 3000 = 600 psi O2

Add 1050 psi He to tank

3000 - 1050 = 1950 psi left over
600 / 1950 = 0.30769
((0.30769 - 0.28) / 0.72) * 1950 = 74.99 psi O2

Add 75 psi O2 and top up to 3000 with EAN28

5: Mix 19/40 with helium containing 2% Oxygen

Want
0.40 * 3000 = 1200 psi He
0.19 * 3000 = 570 psi O2

Need
1200 / 0.98 = 1224.48 psi He

Add 1225 psi He (2/98) to tank

0.02 * 1225 = 24.5 psi O2
570 - 25 = 545 psi O2
3000 - 1225 = 1775 psi left over
545 / 1775 = 0.30704
((0.30704 - 0.21) / 0.79) * 1775 = 218.03 psi O2

Add 218 psi O2 to tank and fill to 3000 psi with air

Answers for chapter 4

1: Fill 10/50 @ 3000 psi

Want
0.5 * 3000 = 1500 psi He

Add 1500 psi He to cylinder and top up to 3000 psi with air

2: How much air do you need to have a 15% O2 mix and what would the Helium% be? (3000 psi)

Want
0.15 * 3000 = 450 psi O2
450 / 0.21 = 2142.85 psi of air needed

3000 - 2143 = 857 psi He
857 / 3000 = 0.285 or 28.5% He

The mix would be 15/28.5

Answers for chapter 5

1: Blend 18/82 Heliox

0.82 * 3000 = 2460 psi He
0.18 * 3000 = 540 psi O2

Add 2460 psi He to tank, then add 540 psi O2 to tank

2: Blend 40/60 Heliox

0.60 * 3000 = 1800 psi He
0.40 * 3000 = 1200 psi O2

Add 1800 psi He, then add 1200 psi O2

Answers for chapter 7

What is in the loop of a mix of 8/60 with 1.3 PPO2 at 330 ft? In addition, what is the END?

330 / 33 = 10 + 1 = 11 ata
1.3 PPO2 / 11 ata = 11.818% O2 (rounded to 11.82% O2)

100 – 11.82 = 88.18% for the rest of the gas

Actual Helium =
((Loop% - O2%) * original He%)
(Original He% + original N2%)

Actual He
= (88.18 * 60) / (60 + 32)
= 57.5% Helium

Actual N2 would be
100 - (11.82 + 57.5) = 30.67% N2

The mix will be 11.82/57.5

N2 and O2 narcosis = ((1 - 0.575) * 11 * 33)) - (33) = 121.275 ft

He narcosis = ((0.235 * 0.575 * 11) * 33) – 33 = 16.05 ft

Total narcosis = 137 ft

Chapter 10

Volume calculations

For billing or stock take purposes, you may need to be able to calculate the amount of gas that was added to fill the tanks.

There are two ways of expressing cylinder sizes, one is to give the free liter size of the cylinder, and the second is to give the volume of gas the cylinder was designed to hold.

Free liters

For free liter sizes, a cylinder will be expressed normally in liters and is the volume of gas the cylinder holds per atmosphere of pressure, or if filled with water the amount of water it will hold.

If you are working in bar then the calculations are easy, just multiply the bar pressure with the free liters given for the cylinder.

Free liter pressure to gas amount formula:
Cylinder size * fill pressure

For example, an 11 L cylinder filled to 200 bar will contain
11 * 200 = 2200 L of gas

For psi to liters it is easier to convert the psi to bar.
1 bar = 14.5037738007 psi

A standard 3000 psi cylinder would be:
3000 / 14.5037738007 = 206.842 bar

Cylinder size

If the cylinder size is given, then you need to know the service rating of the cylinder. A typical size would be 80 cu (cubic) ft that holds 80 cu ft of gas when it is full. The normal service rating pressure is 3000 psi.

Gas volume formula:

$$\frac{(\text{Fill pressure})}{(\text{Service pressure})} * \text{Cylinder size}$$

For example, if you filled a cylinder to 1500 psi the calculation would be:
(1500 / 3000) * 80 = 40 cu ft

To convert backwards and see how much pressure a volume of gas would convert to, do the following calculation:

Free liter to pressure formula:
Gas amount / Cylinder size

Cylinder size to pressure formula:

$$\frac{(\text{Gas amount})}{(\text{Cylinder size})} * \text{Service rating}$$

Free liters example, 400 liters of gas would be:
400 / 11 = 36.36 bar

Cylinder size example would be:
60 cu ft gas in a standard 80 cu ft tank of 3000 psi service rating
(60 / 80) * 3000 = 2250 psi

Chapter 11

Saving a blend

You double and triple checked your numbers, filled the tanks slowly and still things just went wrong; relax, it happens, for there are so many variables at play that it is normal to now and again have an off mix. The reason(s) for the blend being out can be from the tanks not being empty when you started; the left over gas not being what you thought it was; different temperatures of the tanks due to draining, filling or standing in the sun; blending different size tanks together; leaking hoses or valves; faulty gauges; to just human error.

The reason why it happened is only important in helping you to avoid it on the next gas fill, but it does nothing for your current dilemma. The first thing to do is check if your analyzer is reading correctly by calibrating it on a known air tank and rechecking your mix with a different analyzer.

If the mix is found to be off after rechecking, then by how much? Can you still dive the mix or not? If you can dive the mix without radical changes to the dive plan I suggest you leave it as it is. A 1% lower Oxygen content would in most cases not do too much to your decompression schedule, and a 5% difference in helium would affect mostly just the narcosis level but not much in the decompression times.

If you have to change the mix then you most probably will need to drain some gas out and add more helium, Oxygen and air to top it off.

Depending on if the Oxygen, helium or both is low, you are playing a guessing game here. The easier option would be to use a software program to do the calculations for you, but if you do not have one at hand here are some options.

Let's say that you wanted a 20/40 mix and ended up with a 20/35 instead. Here the helium is low and adding any amount of helium will drop your Oxygen content so you will need to add some Oxygen in the end, the question is how much.

We do not want to drain too much, but draining too little will leave us with adding such small amounts of gas that it will be almost impossible to add them.

If you were to decide to drain the mix down to 2500 psi, you will have the following gas in the tanks:

2500 * 0.2 = 500 psi O2
2500 * 0.35 = 875 psi He

You still need
3000 * 0.4 = 1200 psi - 875 = 325 psi He
When adding this to the tank you get 2825 psi in total.

You need 600 psi O2 in total and have 500 psi, thus you still need 100 psi O2. But that O2 needs to be added in the left over space of 3000 - 2825 = 175 psi

The percentage is 100 / 175 = 57.1428
As the air we will top up with contains Oxygen in it we need less than 100 psi O2.
((0.571428 - 0.21) / 0.79) * 175 = 80.06 psi O2

Thus, drain the cylinder to 2500 psi, add 325 psi He and then 80 psi O2 and top up with air.

If you ended with too much helium or Oxygen then you need to see how much you need to drain down to make the amount correct. Let's say you ended with 20/50 and only want 20/40.

The actual total helium you want would be 3000 * 0.4 = 1200 psi

So what would the psi in the tank need to be to make 1200 psi if you have 50% helium in the tank?

Take the total helium needed and divide it by the percentage currently in the tank.

1200 / 0.5 = 2400 psi
Double check 2400 * 0.5 = 1200 psi

From here it is straight forward blending up for we know we have the correct amount of helium and just need to correct the Oxygen.

Total O2 needed is still 600 psi and we have
2400 * 0.2 = 480 psi O2 leaving 600 – 480 = 120 psi O2
120 / 600 = 0.2 this is close to air.

Not surprising as our original Oxygen content was close to air. Since we will only be adding 600 psi of air, the mix will not be affected by much.

600 * 0.21 = 126 psi O2 + 480 = 606 psi O2 total /3000 = 20.2%
Our mix will end up being 20.2/40

With fixing mixes you have to just treat it on a one on one basis and accept that it will happen if you blend enough, especially if you blend in a hurry, and that some days you need to drain all and start from scratch. Just call it school fees and smile. ☺

Chapter 12

Charts:
Nitrox fill chart psi; 100 to 1000

Nitrox Fill Chart Created By Anton Swanepoel										
	100	200	300	400	500	600	700	800	900	1000
22	1	3	4	5	6	8	9	10	11	13
23	3	5	8	10	13	15	18	20	23	25
24	4	8	11	15	19	23	27	30	34	38
25	5	10	15	20	25	30	35	41	46	51
26	6	13	19	25	32	38	44	51	57	63
27	8	15	23	30	38	46	53	61	68	76
28	9	18	27	35	44	53	62	71	80	89
29	10	20	30	41	51	61	71	81	91	101
30	11	23	34	46	57	68	80	91	103	114
31	13	25	38	51	63	76	89	101	114	127
32	14	28	42	56	70	84	97	111	125	139
33	15	30	46	8	76	91	106	122	137	152
34	16	33	49	66	82	99	115	132	19	165
35	18	35	53	71	89	106	124	142	159	177
36	19	38	57	76	95	114	133	152	171	190
37	20	41	61	81	101	122	142	162	182	203
38	22	43	65	86	108	129	151	172	194	215
39	23	46	68	91	114	137	159	182	205	228
40	24	48	72	96	120	144	168	192	216	241
41	25	51	76	101	127	152	177	203	228	253
42	27	53	80	106	133	159	186	213	239	266
43	28	56	84	111	139	167	195	223	251	278
44	29	58	87	116	146	175	204	233	262	291
45	30	61	91	122	152	182	213	243	273	304
46	32	63	95	127	158	190	222	253	285	316
47	33	66	99	132	165	197	230	263	296	329
48	34	68	103	137	171	205	239	273	308	342
49	35	71	106	142	177	213	248	284	319	354
50	37	73	110	147	184	220	257	294	330	367
55	43	86	129	172	215	258	301	344	387	430
60	49	99	148	197	247	296	346	395	444	494
65	56	111	167	223	278	334	390	446	501	557
70	62	124	186	248	310	372	434	496	558	620
75	68	137	205	273	342	410	478	547	615	684
80	75	149	224	299	373	448	523	597	672	747
85	81	162	243	324	405	486	567	648	729	810
90	87	175	262	349	437	524	611	699	786	873
95	94	187	281	375	468	562	656	749	843	937

Nitrox fill chart psi; 1100 to 2000

Nitrox Fill Chart Created By Anton Swanepoel										
	1100	1200	1300	1400	1500	1600	1700	1800	1900	2000
22	14	15	16	18	19	20	22	23	24	25
23	28	30	33	35	38	41	43	46	48	51
24	42	46	49	53	57	61	65	68	72	76
25	56	61	66	71	76	81	86	91	96	101
26	70	76	82	89	95	101	108	114	120	127
27	84	91	99	106	114	122	129	137	144	152
28	97	106	115	124	133	142	151	159	168	177
29	111	122	132	142	152	162	172	182	192	203
30	125	137	148	159	171	182	194	205	216	228
31	139	152	165	177	190	203	215	228	241	253
32	153	167	181	195	209	223	237	251	265	278
33	167	182	197	27	228	243	258	273	289	304
34	181	197	214	230	247	263	280	296	40	329
35	195	213	230	248	266	284	301	319	337	354
36	209	228	247	266	285	304	323	342	361	380
37	223	243	263	284	304	324	344	365	385	405
38	237	258	280	301	323	344	366	387	409	430
39	251	273	296	319	342	365	387	410	433	456
40	265	289	313	337	361	385	409	433	457	481
41	278	304	329	354	380	405	430	456	481	506
42	292	319	346	372	399	425	452	478	505	532
43	306	334	362	390	418	446	473	501	529	557
44	320	349	378	408	437	466	495	524	553	582
45	334	365	395	425	456	486	516	547	577	608
46	348	380	411	443	475	506	538	570	601	633
47	362	395	428	461	494	527	559	592	625	658
48	376	410	444	478	513	547	581	615	649	684
49	390	425	461	496	532	567	603	638	673	709
50	404	441	477	514	551	587	624	661	697	734
55	473	516	559	603	646	689	732	775	818	861
60	543	592	642	691	741	790	839	889	938	987
65	613	668	724	780	835	891	947	1003	1058	1114
70	682	744	806	868	930	992	1054	1116	1178	1241
75	752	820	889	957	1025	1094	1162	1230	1299	1367
80	822	896	971	1046	1120	1195	1270	1344	1419	1494
85	891	972	1053	1134	1215	1296	1377	1458	1539	1620
90	961	1048	1135	1223	1310	1397	1485	1572	1659	1747
95	1030	1124	1218	1311	1405	1499	1592	1686	1780	1873

Nitrox fill chart psi; 2100 to 3000

Nitrox Fill Chart Created By Anton Swanepoel										
	2100	2200	2300	2400	2500	2600	2700	2800	2900	3000
22	27	28	29	30	32	33	34	35	37	38
23	53	56	58	61	63	66	68	71	73	76
24	80	84	87	91	95	99	103	106	110	114
25	106	111	116	122	127	132	137	142	147	152
26	133	139	146	152	158	165	171	177	184	190
27	159	167	175	182	190	197	205	213	220	228
28	186	195	204	213	222	230	239	248	257	266
29	213	223	233	243	253	263	273	284	294	304
30	239	251	262	273	285	296	308	319	330	342
31	266	278	291	304	316	329	342	354	367	380
32	292	306	320	334	348	362	376	390	404	418
33	319	334	349	46	380	395	410	425	441	456
34	346	362	378	395	411	428	444	461	60	494
35	372	390	408	425	443	461	478	496	514	532
36	399	418	437	456	475	494	513	532	551	570
37	425	446	466	486	506	527	547	567	587	608
38	452	473	495	516	538	559	581	603	624	646
39	478	501	524	547	570	592	615	638	661	684
40	505	529	553	577	601	625	649	673	697	722
41	532	557	582	608	633	658	684	709	734	759
42	558	585	611	638	665	691	718	744	771	797
43	585	613	641	668	696	724	752	780	808	835
44	611	641	670	699	728	757	786	815	844	873
45	638	668	699	729	759	790	820	851	881	911
46	665	696	728	759	791	823	854	886	918	949
47	691	724	757	790	823	856	889	922	954	987
48	718	752	786	820	854	889	923	957	991	1025
49	744	780	815	851	886	922	957	992	1028	1063
50	771	808	844	881	918	954	991	1028	1065	1101
55	904	947	990	1033	1076	1119	1162	1205	1248	1291
60	1037	1086	1135	1185	1234	1284	1333	1382	1432	1481
65	1170	1225	1281	1337	1392	1448	1504	1559	1615	1671
70	1303	1365	1427	1489	1551	1613	1675	1737	1799	1861
75	1435	1504	1572	1641	1709	1777	1846	1914	1982	2051
80	1568	1643	1718	1792	1867	1942	2016	2091	2166	2241
85	1701	1782	1863	1944	2025	2106	2187	2268	2349	2430
90	1834	1922	2009	2096	2184	2271	2358	2446	2533	2620
95	1967	2061	2154	2248	2342	2435	2529	2623	2716	2810

Nitrox fill chart psi; 3100 to 4000

Nitrox Fill Chart Created By Anton Swanepoel										
	3100	3200	3300	3400	3500	3600	3700	3800	3900	4000
22	39	41	42	43	44	46	47	48	49	51
23	78	81	84	86	89	91	94	96	99	101
24	118	122	125	129	133	137	141	144	148	152
25	157	162	167	172	177	182	187	192	197	203
26	196	203	209	215	222	228	234	241	247	253
27	235	243	251	258	266	273	281	289	296	304
28	275	284	292	301	310	319	328	337	346	354
29	314	324	334	344	354	365	375	385	395	405
30	353	365	376	387	399	410	422	433	444	456
31	392	405	418	430	443	456	468	481	494	506
32	432	446	459	473	487	501	515	529	543	557
33	471	486	501	65	532	547	562	577	592	608
34	510	527	543	559	576	592	609	625	81	658
35	549	567	585	603	620	638	656	673	691	709
36	589	608	627	646	665	684	703	722	741	759
37	628	648	668	689	709	729	749	770	790	810
38	667	689	710	732	753	775	796	818	839	861
39	706	729	752	775	797	820	843	866	889	911
40	746	770	794	818	842	866	890	914	938	962
41	785	810	835	861	886	911	937	962	987	1013
42	824	851	877	904	930	957	984	1010	1037	1063
43	863	891	919	947	975	1003	1030	1058	1086	1114
44	903	932	961	990	1019	1048	1077	1106	1135	1165
45	942	972	1003	1033	1063	1094	1124	1154	1185	1215
46	981	1013	1044	1076	1108	1139	1171	1203	1234	1266
47	1020	1053	1086	1119	1152	1185	1218	1251	1284	1316
48	1059	1094	1128	1162	1196	1230	1265	1299	1333	1367
49	1099	1134	1170	1205	1241	1276	1311	1347	1382	1418
50	1138	1175	1211	1248	1285	1322	1358	1395	1432	1468
55	1334	1377	1420	1463	1506	1549	1592	1635	1678	1722
60	1530	1580	1629	1678	1728	1777	1827	1876	1925	1975
65	1727	1782	1838	1894	1949	2005	2061	2116	2172	2228
70	1923	1985	2047	2109	2171	2233	2295	2357	2419	2481
75	2119	2187	2256	2324	2392	2461	2529	2597	2666	2734
80	2315	2390	2465	2539	2614	2689	2763	2838	2913	2987
85	2511	2592	2673	2754	2835	2916	2997	3078	3159	3241
90	2708	2795	2882	2970	3057	3144	3232	3319	3406	3494
95	2904	2997	3091	3185	3278	3372	3466	3559	3653	3747

Nitrox fill chart bar; 10 to 100

Nitrox Fill Chart Created By Anton Swanepoel										
	10	20	30	40	50	60	70	80	90	100
22	0	0	0	1	1	1	1	1	1	1
23	0	1	1	1	1	2	2	2	2	3
24	0	1	1	2	2	2	3	3	3	4
25	1	1	2	2	3	3	4	4	5	5
26	1	1	2	3	3	4	4	5	6	6
27	1	2	2	3	4	5	5	6	7	8
28	1	2	3	4	4	5	6	7	8	9
29	1	2	3	4	5	6	7	8	9	10
30	1	2	3	5	6	7	8	9	10	11
31	1	3	4	5	6	8	9	10	11	13
32	1	3	4	6	7	8	10	11	13	14
33	2	3	5	1	8	9	11	12	14	15
34	2	3	5	7	8	10	12	13	2	16
35	2	4	5	7	9	11	12	14	16	18
36	2	4	6	8	9	11	13	15	17	19
37	2	4	6	8	10	12	14	16	18	20
38	2	4	6	9	11	13	15	17	19	22
39	2	5	7	9	11	14	16	18	21	23
40	2	5	7	10	12	14	17	19	22	24
41	3	5	8	10	13	15	18	20	23	25
42	3	5	8	11	13	16	19	21	24	27
43	3	6	8	11	14	17	19	22	25	28
44	3	6	9	12	15	17	20	23	26	29
45	3	6	9	12	15	18	21	24	27	30
46	3	6	9	13	16	19	22	25	28	32
47	3	7	10	13	16	20	23	26	30	33
48	3	7	10	14	17	21	24	27	31	34
49	4	7	11	14	18	21	25	28	32	35
50	4	7	11	15	18	22	26	29	33	37
55	4	9	13	17	22	26	30	34	39	43
60	5	10	15	20	25	30	35	39	44	49
65	6	11	17	22	28	33	39	45	50	56
70	6	12	19	25	31	37	43	50	56	62
75	7	14	21	27	34	41	48	55	62	68
80	7	15	22	30	37	45	52	60	67	75
85	8	16	24	32	41	49	57	65	73	81
90	9	17	26	35	44	52	61	70	79	87
95	9	19	28	37	47	56	66	75	84	94

Nitrox fill chart bar; 110 to 200

Nitrox Fill Chart Created By Anton Swanepoel										
	110	120	130	140	150	160	170	180	190	200
22	1	2	2	2	2	2	2	2	2	3
23	3	3	3	4	4	4	4	5	5	5
24	4	5	5	5	6	6	6	7	7	8
25	6	6	7	7	8	8	9	9	10	10
26	7	8	8	9	9	10	11	11	12	13
27	8	9	10	11	11	12	13	14	14	15
28	10	11	12	12	13	14	15	16	17	18
29	11	12	13	14	15	16	17	18	19	20
30	13	14	15	16	17	18	19	21	22	23
31	14	15	16	18	19	20	22	23	24	25
32	15	17	18	19	21	22	24	25	26	28
33	17	18	20	3	23	24	26	27	29	30
34	18	20	21	23	25	26	28	30	4	33
35	19	21	23	25	27	28	30	32	34	35
36	21	23	25	27	28	30	32	34	36	38
37	22	24	26	28	30	32	34	36	38	41
38	24	26	28	30	32	34	37	39	41	43
39	25	27	30	32	34	36	39	41	43	46
40	26	29	31	34	36	38	41	43	46	48
41	28	30	33	35	38	41	43	46	48	51
42	29	32	35	37	40	43	45	48	51	53
43	31	33	36	39	42	45	47	50	53	56
44	32	35	38	41	44	47	49	52	55	58
45	33	36	39	43	46	49	52	55	58	61
46	35	38	41	44	47	51	54	57	60	63
47	36	39	43	46	49	53	56	59	63	66
48	38	41	44	48	51	55	58	62	65	68
49	39	43	46	50	53	57	60	64	67	71
50	40	44	48	51	55	59	62	66	70	73
55	47	52	56	60	65	69	73	77	82	86
60	54	59	64	69	74	79	84	89	94	99
65	61	67	72	78	84	89	95	100	106	111
70	68	74	81	87	93	99	105	112	118	124
75	75	82	89	96	103	109	116	123	130	137
80	82	90	97	105	112	119	127	134	142	149
85	89	97	105	113	122	130	138	146	154	162
90	96	105	114	122	131	140	148	157	166	175
95	103	112	122	131	141	150	159	169	178	187

Nitrox fill chart bar; 210 to 300

Nitrox Fill Chart Created By Anton Swanepoel

	210	220	230	240	250	260	270	280	290	300
22	3	3	3	3	3	3	3	4	4	4
23	5	6	6	6	6	7	7	7	7	8
24	8	8	9	9	9	10	10	11	11	11
25	11	11	12	12	13	13	14	14	15	15
26	13	14	15	15	16	16	17	18	18	19
27	16	17	17	18	19	20	21	21	22	23
28	19	19	20	21	22	23	24	25	26	27
29	21	22	23	24	25	26	27	28	29	30
30	24	25	26	27	28	30	31	32	33	34
31	27	28	29	30	32	33	34	35	37	38
32	29	31	32	33	35	36	38	39	40	42
33	32	33	35	5	38	39	41	43	44	46
34	35	36	38	39	41	43	44	46	6	49
35	37	39	41	43	44	46	48	50	51	53
36	40	42	44	46	47	49	51	53	55	57
37	43	45	47	49	51	53	55	57	59	61
38	45	47	49	52	54	56	58	60	62	65
39	48	50	52	55	57	59	62	64	66	68
40	51	53	55	58	60	63	65	67	70	72
41	53	56	58	61	63	66	68	71	73	76
42	56	58	61	64	66	69	72	74	77	80
43	58	61	64	67	70	72	75	78	81	84
44	61	64	67	70	73	76	79	82	84	87
45	64	67	70	73	76	79	82	85	88	91
46	66	70	73	76	79	82	85	89	92	95
47	69	72	76	79	82	86	89	92	95	99
48	72	75	79	82	85	89	92	96	99	103
49	74	78	82	85	89	92	96	99	103	106
50	77	81	84	88	92	95	99	103	106	110
55	90	95	99	103	108	112	116	121	125	129
60	104	109	114	118	123	128	133	138	143	148
65	117	123	128	134	139	145	150	156	162	167
70	130	136	143	149	155	161	167	174	180	186
75	144	150	157	164	171	178	185	191	198	205
80	157	164	172	179	187	194	202	209	217	224
85	170	178	186	194	203	211	219	227	235	243
90	183	192	201	210	218	227	236	245	253	262
95	197	206	215	225	234	244	253	262	272	281

Helair fill chart psi

Amounts given are for Helium gas to be added.

Helair Fill Chart Created By Anton Swanepoel

	250	500	750	1000	1250	1500	1750	2000	2250	2500	2750	3000	3250	3500
1/95	237.5	475	712.5	950	1187.5	1425	1662.5	1900	2137.5	2375	2612.5	2850	3087.5	3325
2/90	225	450	675	900	1125	1350	1575	1800	2025	2250	2475	2700	2925	3150
3/85	212.5	425	637.5	850	1062.5	1275	1487.5	1700	1912.5	2125	2337.5	2550	2762.5	2975
4/80	200	400	600	800	1000	1200	1400	1600	1800	2000	2200	2400	2600	2800
5/75	187.5	375	562.5	750	937.5	1125	1312.5	1500	1687.5	1875	2062.5	2250	2437.5	2625
6/70	175	350	525	700	875	1050	1225	1400	1575	1750	1925	2100	2275	2450
7/65	162.5	325	487.5	650	812.5	975	1137.5	1300	1462.5	1625	1787.5	1950	2112.5	2275
8/60	150	300	450	600	750	900	1050	1200	1350	1500	1650	1800	1950	2100
9/55	137.5	275	412.5	550	687.5	825	962.5	1100	1237.5	1375	1512.5	1650	1787.5	1925
10/50	125	250	375	500	625	750	875	1000	1125	1250	1375	1500	1625	1750
11/45	112.5	225	337.5	450	562.5	675	787.5	900	1012.5	1125	1237.5	1350	1462.5	1575
12/40	100	200	300	400	500	600	700	800	900	1000	1100	1200	1300	1400
13/35	87.5	175	262.5	350	437.5	525	612.5	700	787.5	875	962.5	1050	1137.5	1225
15/30	75	150	225	300	375	450	525	600	675	750	825	900	975	1050
16/25	62.5	125	187.5	250	312.5	375	437.5	500	562.5	625	687.5	750	812.5	875
17/20	50	100	150	200	250	300	350	400	450	500	550	600	650	700
18/15	37.5	75	112.5	150	187.5	225	262.5	300	337.5	375	412.5	450	487.5	525
19/10	25	50	75	100	125	150	175	200	225	250	275	300	325	350
20/5	12.5	25	37.5	50	62.5	75	87.5	100	112.5	125	137.5	150	162.5	175

Helair fill chart bar

Helair Fill Chart Created By Anton Swanepoel

	20	40	60	100	120	140	160	200	220	240	260	280	300	320
1/95	19	38	57	95	114	133	152	190	209	228	247	266	285	304
2/90	18	36	54	90	108	126	144	180	198	216	234	252	270	288
3/85	17	34	51	85	102	119	136	170	187	204	221	238	255	272
4/80	16	32	48	80	96	112	128	160	176	192	208	224	240	256
5/75	15	30	45	75	90	105	120	150	165	180	195	210	225	240
6/70	14	28	42	70	84	98	112	140	154	168	182	196	210	224
7/65	13	26	39	65	78	91	104	130	143	156	169	182	195	208
8/60	12	24	36	60	72	84	96	120	132	144	156	168	180	192
9/55	11	22	33	55	66	77	88	110	121	132	143	154	165	176
10/50	10	20	30	50	60	70	80	100	110	120	130	140	150	160
11/45	9	18	27	45	54	63	72	90	99	108	117	126	135	144
12/40	8	16	24	40	48	56	64	80	88	96	104	112	120	128
13/35	7	14	21	35	42	49	56	70	77	84	91	98	105	112
15/30	6	12	18	30	36	42	48	60	66	72	78	84	90	96
16/25	5	10	15	25	30	35	40	50	55	60	65	70	75	80
17/20	4	8	12	20	24	28	32	40	44	48	52	56	60	64
18/15	3	6	9	15	18	21	24	30	33	36	39	42	45	48
19/10	2	4	6	10	12	14	16	20	22	24	26	28	30	32
20/5	1	2	3	5	6	7	8	10	11	12	13	14	15	16

Tri-Mix fill chart psi

Top line is Helium and bottom line is O2.

Tri Mix Fill Chart Created By Anton Swanepoel															
	250	500	750	1000	1250	1500	1750	2000	2250	2500	2750	3000	3250	3500	3750
8/80	200.0	400.0	600.0	800.0	1000.0	1200.0	1400.0	1600.0	1800.0	2000.0	2200.0	2400.0	2600.0	2800.0	3000.0
	12.0	24.1	36.1	48.1	60.1	72.2	84.2	96.2	108.2	120.3	132.3	144.3	156.3	168.4	180.4
9/75	187.5	375.0	562.5	750.0	937.5	1125.0	1312.5	1500.0	1687.5	1875.0	2062.5	2250.0	2437.5	2625.0	2812.5
	11.9	23.7	35.6	47.5	59.3	71.2	83.1	94.9	106.8	118.7	130.5	142.4	154.3	166.1	178.0
10/65	162.5	325.0	487.5	650.0	812.5	975.0	1137.5	1300.0	1462.5	1625.0	1787.5	1950.0	2112.5	2275.0	2437.5
	8.4	16.8	25.2	33.5	41.9	50.3	58.7	67.1	75.5	83.9	92.2	100.6	109.0	117.4	125.8
10/80	200.0	400.0	600.0	800.0	1000.0	1200.0	1400.0	1600.0	1800.0	2000.0	2200.0	2400.0	2600.0	2800.0	3000.0
	18.4	36.7	55.1	73.4	91.8	110.1	128.5	146.8	165.2	183.5	201.9	220.3	238.6	257.0	275.3
12/55	137.5	275.0	412.5	550.0	687.5	825.0	962.5	1100.0	1237.5	1375.0	1512.5	1650.0	1787.5	1925.0	2062.5
	8.1	16.1	24.2	32.3	40.3	48.4	56.5	64.6	72.6	80.7	88.8	96.8	104.9	113.0	121.0
12/75	187.5	375.0	562.5	750.0	937.5	1125.0	1312.5	1500.0	1687.5	1875.0	2062.5	2250.0	2437.5	2625.0	2812.5
	21.4	42.7	64.1	85.4	106.8	128.2	149.5	170.9	192.2	213.6	235.0	256.3	277.7	299.1	320.4
13/70	175.0	350.0	525.0	700.0	875.0	1050.0	1225.0	1400.0	1575.0	1750.0	1925.0	2100.0	2275.0	2450.0	2625.0
	21.2	42.4	63.6	84.8	106.0	127.2	148.4	169.6	190.8	212.0	233.2	254.4	275.6	296.8	318.0
14/44	110.0	220.0	330.0	440.0	550.0	660.0	770.0	880.0	990.0	1100.0	1210.0	1320.0	1430.0	1540.0	1650.0
	7.1	14.2	21.3	28.4	35.4	42.5	49.6	56.7	63.8	70.9	78.0	85.1	92.2	99.2	106.3
14/65	162.5	325.0	487.5	650.0	812.5	975.0	1137.5	1300.0	1462.5	1625.0	1787.5	1950.0	2112.5	2275.0	2437.5
	21.0	42.1	63.1	84.2	105.2	126.3	147.3	168.4	189.4	210.4	231.5	252.5	273.6	294.6	315.7
16/55	137.5	275.0	412.5	550.0	687.5	825.0	962.5	1100.0	1237.5	1375.0	1512.5	1650.0	1787.5	1925.0	2062.5
	20.7	41.5	62.2	82.9	103.6	124.4	145.1	165.8	186.6	207.3	228.0	248.7	269.5	290.2	310.9
18/35	87.5	175.0	262.5	350.0	437.5	525.0	612.5	700.0	787.5	875.0	962.5	1050.0	1137.5	1225.0	1312.5
	13.8	27.5	41.3	55.1	68.8	82.6	96.4	110.1	123.9	137.7	151.4	165.2	179.0	192.7	206.5
18/40	100.0	200.0	300.0	400.0	500.0	600.0	700.0	800.0	900.0	1000.0	1100.0	1200.0	1300.0	1400.0	1500.0
	17.1	34.2	51.3	68.4	85.4	102.5	119.6	136.7	153.8	170.9	188.0	205.1	222.2	239.2	256.3
20/40	100.0	200.0	300.0	400.0	500.0	600.0	700.0	800.0	900.0	1000.0	1100.0	1200.0	1300.0	1400.0	1500.0
	23.4	46.8	70.3	93.7	117.1	140.5	163.9	187.3	210.8	234.2	257.6	281.0	304.4	327.8	351.3
20/35	87.5	175.0	262.5	350.0	437.5	525.0	612.5	700.0	787.5	875.0	962.5	1050.0	1137.5	1225.0	1312.5
	20.1	40.2	60.3	80.4	100.5	120.6	140.7	160.8	180.9	200.9	221.0	241.1	261.2	281.3	301.4
24/30	75.0	150.0	225.0	300.0	375.0	450.0	525.0	600.0	675.0	750.0	825.0	900.0	975.0	1050.0	1125.0
	29.4	58.9	88.3	117.7	147.2	176.6	206.0	235.4	264.9	294.3	323.7	353.2	382.6	412.0	441.5
32/20	50.0	100.0	150.0	200.0	250.0	300.0	350.0	400.0	450.0	500.0	550.0	600.0	650.0	700.0	750.0
	48.1	96.2	144.3	192.4	240.5	288.6	336.7	384.8	432.9	481.0	529.1	577.2	625.3	673.4	721.5
40/20	50.0	100.0	150.0	200.0	250.0	300.0	350.0	400.0	450.0	500.0	550.0	600.0	650.0	700.0	750.0
	73.4	146.8	220.3	293.7	367.1	440.5	513.9	587.3	660.8	734.2	807.6	881.0	954.4	1027.8	1101.3
50/20	50.0	100.0	150.0	200.0	250.0	300.0	350.0	400.0	450.0	500.0	550.0	600.0	650.0	700.0	750.0
	105.1	210.1	315.2	420.3	525.3	630.4	735.4	840.5	945.6	1050.6	1155.7	1260.8	1365.8	1470.9	1575.9
60/20	50.0	100.0	150.0	200.0	250.0	300.0	350.0	400.0	450.0	500.0	550.0	600.0	650.0	700.0	750.0
	136.7	273.4	410.1	546.8	683.5	820.3	957.0	1093.7	1230.4	1367.1	1503.8	1640.5	1777.2	1913.9	2050.6

Tri-Mix fill chart bar

Tri Mix Fill Chart Created By Anton Swanepoel															
	20	40	60	80	100	120	140	160	180	200	220	240	260	280	300
8/80	16.0	32.0	48.0	64.0	80.0	96.0	112.0	128.0	144.0	160.0	176.0	192.0	208.0	224.0	240.0
	1.0	1.9	2.9	3.8	4.8	5.8	6.7	7.7	8.7	9.6	10.6	11.5	12.5	13.5	14.4
9/75	15.0	30.0	45.0	60.0	75.0	90.0	105.0	120.0	135.0	150.0	165.0	180.0	195.0	210.0	225.0
	0.9	1.9	2.8	3.8	4.7	5.7	6.6	7.6	8.5	9.5	10.4	11.4	12.3	13.3	14.2
10/65	13.0	26.0	39.0	52.0	65.0	78.0	91.0	104.0	117.0	130.0	143.0	156.0	169.0	182.0	195.0
	0.7	1.3	2.0	2.7	3.4	4.0	4.7	5.4	6.0	6.7	7.4	8.1	8.7	9.4	10.1
10/80	16.0	32.0	48.0	64.0	80.0	96.0	112.0	128.0	144.0	160.0	176.0	192.0	208.0	224.0	240.0
	1.5	2.9	4.4	5.9	7.3	8.8	10.3	11.7	13.2	14.7	16.2	17.6	19.1	20.6	22.0
12/55	11.0	22.0	33.0	44.0	55.0	66.0	77.0	88.0	99.0	110.0	121.0	132.0	143.0	154.0	165.0
	0.6	1.3	1.9	2.6	3.2	3.9	4.5	5.2	5.8	6.5	7.1	7.7	8.4	9.0	9.7
12/75	15.0	30.0	45.0	60.0	75.0	90.0	105.0	120.0	135.0	150.0	165.0	180.0	195.0	210.0	225.0
	1.7	3.4	5.1	6.8	8.5	10.3	12.0	13.7	15.4	17.1	18.8	20.5	22.2	23.9	25.6
13/70	14.0	28.0	42.0	56.0	70.0	84.0	98.0	112.0	126.0	140.0	154.0	168.0	182.0	196.0	210.0
	1.7	3.4	5.1	6.8	8.5	10.2	11.9	13.6	15.3	17.0	18.7	20.4	22.1	23.7	25.4
14/44	8.8	17.6	26.4	35.2	44.0	52.8	61.6	70.4	79.2	88.0	96.8	105.6	114.4	123.2	132.0
	0.6	1.1	1.7	2.3	2.8	3.4	4.0	4.5	5.1	5.7	6.2	6.8	7.4	7.9	8.5
14/65	13.0	26.0	39.0	52.0	65.0	78.0	91.0	104.0	117.0	130.0	143.0	156.0	169.0	182.0	195.0
	1.7	3.4	5.1	6.7	8.4	10.1	11.8	13.5	15.2	16.8	18.5	20.2	21.9	23.6	25.3
16/55	11.0	22.0	33.0	44.0	55.0	66.0	77.0	88.0	99.0	110.0	121.0	132.0	143.0	154.0	165.0
	1.7	3.3	5.0	6.6	8.3	9.9	11.6	13.3	14.9	16.6	18.2	19.9	21.6	23.2	24.9
18/35	7.0	14.0	21.0	28.0	35.0	42.0	49.0	56.0	63.0	70.0	77.0	84.0	91.0	98.0	105.0
	1.1	2.2	3.3	4.4	5.5	6.6	7.7	8.8	9.9	11.0	12.1	13.2	14.3	15.4	16.5
18/40	8.0	16.0	24.0	32.0	40.0	48.0	56.0	64.0	72.0	80.0	88.0	96.0	104.0	112.0	120.0
	1.4	2.7	4.1	5.5	6.8	8.2	9.6	10.9	12.3	13.7	15.0	16.4	17.8	19.1	20.5
20/40	8.0	16.0	24.0	32.0	40.0	48.0	56.0	64.0	72.0	80.0	88.0	96.0	104.0	112.0	120.0
	1.9	3.7	5.6	7.5	9.4	11.2	13.1	15.0	16.9	18.7	20.6	22.5	24.4	26.2	28.1
20/35	7.0	14.0	21.0	28.0	35.0	42.0	49.0	56.0	63.0	70.0	77.0	84.0	91.0	98.0	105.0
	1.6	3.2	4.8	6.4	8.0	9.6	11.3	12.9	14.5	16.1	17.7	19.3	20.9	22.5	24.1
24/30	6.0	12.0	18.0	24.0	30.0	36.0	42.0	48.0	54.0	60.0	66.0	72.0	78.0	84.0	90.0
	2.4	4.7	7.1	9.4	11.8	14.1	16.5	18.8	21.2	23.5	25.9	28.3	30.6	33.0	35.3
32/20	4.0	8.0	12.0	16.0	20.0	24.0	28.0	32.0	36.0	40.0	44.0	48.0	52.0	56.0	60.0
	3.8	7.7	11.5	15.4	19.2	23.1	26.9	30.8	34.6	38.5	42.3	46.2	50.0	53.9	57.7
40/20	4.0	8.0	12.0	16.0	20.0	24.0	28.0	32.0	36.0	40.0	44.0	48.0	52.0	56.0	60.0
	5.9	11.7	17.6	23.5	29.4	35.2	41.1	47.0	52.9	58.7	64.6	70.5	76.4	82.2	88.1
50/20	4.0	8.0	12.0	16.0	20.0	24.0	28.0	32.0	36.0	40.0	44.0	48.0	52.0	56.0	60.0
	8.4	16.8	25.2	33.6	42.0	50.4	58.8	67.2	75.6	84.1	92.5	100.9	109.3	117.7	126.1
60/20	4.0	8.0	12.0	16.0	20.0	24.0	28.0	32.0	36.0	40.0	44.0	48.0	52.0	56.0	60.0
	10.9	21.9	32.8	43.7	54.7	65.6	76.6	87.5	98.4	109.4	120.3	131.2	142.2	153.1	164.1

EAD chart Feet

EAD Chart Feet By Anton Swanepoel																													
	40	45	50	55	60	65	70	75	80	85	90	95	100	105	110	115	120	125	130	135	140	145	150	155	160	165	170	175	180
22	39	44	49	54	59	64	69	74	79	84	88	93	98	103	108	113	118	123	128	133	138	143	148	153	158	162	167	172	177
23	38	43	48	53	58	63	67	72	77	82	87	92	97	102	106	111	116	121	126	131	136	140	145	150	155	160	165	170	175
24	36	41	47	52	56	61	66	71	76	81	85	90	95	100	105	109	114	119	124	129	133	138	143	148	153	157	162	167	172
25	36	41	46	51	55	60	65	70	74	79	84	89	93	98	103	108	112	117	122	126	131	136	141	145	150	155	160	164	
26	35	40	45	49	54	59	63	68	73	78	82	87	92	96	101	106	110	115	120	124	129	134	138	143	148	152	157		
27	34	39	44	48	53	58	62	67	71	76	81	85	90	95	99	104	108	113	118	122	127	131	136	141	145				
28	34	38	43	47	52	56	61	65	70	75	79	84	88	93	97	102	106	111	116	120	125	129	134	138					
29	33	37	42	46	51	55	60	23	69	73	78	82	87	91	96	100	105	109	113	118	122	127							
30	32	36	41	45	49	54	58	63	67	72	76	80	85	89	94	98	103	107	111	116	120								
31	31	35	39	44	48	53	57	61	66	70	74	79	83	88	92	96	101	105	109	114									
32	30	34	38	43	47	51	56	60	64	69	73	77	81	86	90	94	99	103	107										
33	29	33	37	42	46	50	54	59	63	67	71	76	80	84	88	93	97	101											
34	28	32	36	41	45	49	53	57	61	66	70	74	78	82	86	91	95												
35	27	31	35	39	44	48	52	56	60	64	68	72	76	81	85	89													
36	26	30	34	38	42	46	50	54	59	63	67	71	75	79	83														
37	25	29	33	37	41	45	49	53	57	61	65	69	73	77	81														
38	24	28	32	36	40	44	48	52	56	60	64	67	71	75															
39	23	27	31	35	39	43	47	50	54	58	62	66	70																
40	22	26	30	34	38	41	45	49	53	57	60	64																	
45	18	21	25	28	32	35	39	42	46																				
50	13	16	20	23	26	29	32																						
55	9	11	14	17	20	23																							
60	4	6	9	12																									

EAD chart meters

EAD Chart Meters By Anton Swanepoel

	15	16	17	18	19	20	21	22	23	24	25	26	27	28	29	30	32	34	36	38	40	42	44	46	48	50	52	54	56
22	15	16	17	18	19	20	21	22	23	24	25	26	27	28	29	29	31	33	35	37	39	41	43	45	47	49	51	53	55
23	14	15	16	17	18	19	20	21	22	23	24	25	26	27	28	29	31	33	35	37	39	41	43	45	47	48	50	52	54
24	14	15	16	17	18	19	20	21	22	23	24	25	26	27	28	28	30	32	34	36	38	40	42	44	46	48	50	52	53
25	14	15	16	17	18	18	19	20	21	22	23	24	25	26	27	28	30	32	34	36	37	39	41	43	45	47	49	51	
26	13	14	15	16	17	18	19	20	21	22	23	24	25	26	27	27	29	31	33	35	37	39	41	42	44	46	48		
27	13	14	15	16	17	18	19	20	20	21	22	23	24	25	26	27	29	31	33	34	36	38	40	42	44				
28	13	14	15	16	16	17	18	19	20	21	22	23	24	25	26	26	28	30	32	34	36	37	39	41					
29	12	13	14	15	16	17	18	25	20	21	21	22	23	24	25	26	28	30	31	33	35	37							
30	12	13	14	15	16	17	17	18	19	20	21	22	23	24	25	25	27	29	31	33	34								
31	12	13	14	14	15	16	17	18	19	20	21	21	22	23	24	25	27	28	30	32									
32	12	12	13	14	15	16	17	18	18	19	20	21	22	23	24	24	26	28	30										
33	11	12	13	14	15	15	16	17	18	19	20	21	21	22	23	24	26	27											
34	11	12	13	13	14	15	16	17	18	18	19	20	21	22	23	23	25												
35	11	11	12	13	14	15	16	16	17	18	19	20	20	21	22	23													
36	10	11	12	13	13	14	15	16	17	18	18	19	20	21	22														
37	10	11	12	12	13	14	15	16	16	17	18	19	20	20	21														
38	10	10	11	12	13	14	14	15	16	17	17	18	19	20															
39	9	10	11	12	12	13	14	15	15	16	17	18	19																
40	9	10	11	11	12	13	14	14	15	16	17	17																	
45	7	8	9	9	10	11	12	12	13																				
50	6	6	7	8	8	9	10																						
55	4	5	5	6	7	7																							
60	3	3	4	4																									

END chart feet

END Tri-Mix Open Circuit Chart Feet Created by Anton Swanepoel																
	100	120	140	160	180	200	220	240	260	280	300	330	350	400	450	500
8/80	0	0	2	9	17	24	32	40	48	55	63	75	83	102	121	141
8/60	20	28	36	44	52	60	71	82	93	103	114	130	141	168	195	222
9/75	0	5	10	16	25	33	42	50	59	67	76	89	97	118	140	161
9/55	27	36	45	54	63	72	81	92	104	115	127	144	156	185	214	243
10/80	0	0	2	9	17	24	32	40	48	55	63	75	83	102	121	141
10/65	14	21	28	35	42	51	61	71	81	91	101	117	127	152	177	202
10/50	34	44	54	64	74	84	94	104	115	127	140	158	171	201	232	263
11/45	40	51	62	73	84	95	106	117	128	139	152	172	185	218	251	
12/75	0	5	10	16	25	33	42	50	59	67	76	89	97	118		
12/60	20	28	36	44	52	60	71	82	93	103	114	130	141	168		
12/55	27	36	45	54	63	72	81	92	104	115	127	144	156	185		
13/70	7	13	19	25	33	42	52	61	70	79	89	103	112			
13/50	34	44	54	64	74	84	94	104	115	127	140	158	171			
13/38	63	77	92	106	120	135	149	164	178	192	207	228	243			
14/65	14	21	28	35	42	51	61	71	81	91	101	117	127			
14/44	42	53	64	75	86	98	109	120	131	142	155	174	188			
14/33	56	70	83	96	110	123	137	150	163	177	190	210	224			
15/28	63	77	92	106	120	135	149	164	178	192	207					
16/55	27	34	45	54	63	72	81	92	104	115	127					
16/24	68	83	99	114	129	144	159	175	190	205	220					
17/60	20	28	36	44	52	60	71	82	93	103						
17/19	75	91	107	123	140	155	172	188	204	221						
18/40	47	59	71	83	95	107	119	131	143							
18/35	54	67	80	93	106	119	132	145	158							
20/40	47	59	71	83	95	107	119	131								
20/35	54	67	80	93	106	119	132	145								
24/30	60	74	88	102	116											
32/30	60	74	88													
32/20	73	89	106													

END chart meters

END Tri-Mix Open Circuit Chart Meters Created by Anton Swanepoel

	31	37	43	49	55	61	67	73	79	85	90	100	106	122	137	152
8/80	0	0	0	3	5	7	10	12	14	17	19	22	25	31	37	43
8/60	6	9	11	14	16	18	21	25	28	31	34	39	42	51	59	67
9/75	0	2	3	5	7	10	13	15	18	20	22	27	29	36	42	49
9/55	8	11	14	16	19	22	25	28	31	35	38	43	47	56	65	74
10/80	0	0	0	3	5	7	10	12	14	17	19	22	25	31	37	43
10/65	4	6	8	11	13	15	18	21	24	27	30	36	38	46	54	61
10/50	10	13	16	19	22	25	28	31	35	38	42	48	51	61	71	80
11/45	13	16	19	22	26	29	32	36	39	42	45	52	56	66	76	
12/75	0	2	3	5	7	10	13	15	18	20	22	27	29	37		
12/60	6	9	11	14	16	18	21	25	28	31	34	39	42	51		
12/55	8	11	14	16	19	22	25	28	31	35	38	43	47	56		
13/70	2	4	6	8	10	13	15	18	21	24	26	31	34			
13/50	10	13	16	19	22	25	28	31	35	38	42	48	51			
13/38	15	19	23	27	30	34	38	41	45	49	52	58	62			
14/65	4	6	8	11	13	15	18	21	24	27	30	35	38			
14/44	13	16	20	23	26	30	33	36	40	43	46	53	57			
14/33	17	21	25	30	34	38	42	46	50	54	57	64	68			
15/28	20	24	28	32	37	41	45	50	54	58	62					
16/55	8	11	14	16	19	22	25	28	31	35	38					
16/24	21	26	30	35	39	44	49	53	58	62	66					
17/60	6	9	11	14	16	18	21	25	28	31						
17/19	23	28	33	38	43	48	52	57	62	67						
18/40	15	18	22	25	29	33	36	40	43							
18/35	17	21	24	28	33	36	40	44	48							
20/40	15	18	22	25	29	33	36	40								
20/35	17	21	24	28	32	36	40	44								
24/30	19	23	27	31	35											
32/30	19	23	27													
32/20	23	28	33													

Best gas

Note: Mixes in darker highlight can be obtained or a close match using Helair mixes. PPO2 are as close to the PPO2 wanted for the depth, some may exceed the value slightly, but at a very small amount as choosing a lower O2% would drop the O2% to far away from the desired value. Values that exceed 1.6 are for gas switching at optimum PPO2.

Best gas feet

Best gas Chart Feet Created By Anton Swanepoel															
Depth Feet	60	70	80	90	100	110	120	130	140	150	160	170	180	190	200
PPO2 @1	35	32	29	27	25	23	21	20	19	18	17	16	15	14	14
PPO2 @1.3	46	41	38	35	32	30	28	26	24	23	22	21	20	19	18
PPO2 @1.4	49	44	40	37	34	32	30	28	26	25	24	22	21	20	19
PPO2 @1.5	53	48	43	40	37	34	32	30	28	27	25	24	23	22	21
PPO2 @1.6	56	51	46	43	39	37	34	32	30	29	27	26	24	23	22
END 100FT PPO2 @1					25	23/7	21/13	20/19	19/23	18/28	17/31	16/35	15/38	14/41	14/43
END 100 FT PPO2 @ 1.3					32	30/7	28/13	26/19	24/23	23/28	22/31	21/35	20/38	19/41	18/43
END 100 FT PPO2 @ 1.4					34	32/7	30/13	28/19	26/23	25/28	24/31	22/35	21/38	20/41	19/43
END 100 FT PPO2 @ 1.6					39	37/7	34/13	32/19	30/23	29/28	27/31	26/35	24/38	23/41	22/43
END 130FT PPO2 @1								20	19/6	18/11	17/16	16/20	15/24	14/27	14/30
END 130 FT PPO2 @ 1.3								26	24/6	23/11	22/16	21/20	20/24	19/27	18/30
END 130 FT PPO2 @ 1.4								28	26/6	25/11	24/16	22/20	21/24	20/27	19/30
END 130 FT PPO2 @ 1.6								32	30/6	29/11	27/16	26/20	24/24	23/27	22/30

Depth Feet	210	220	240	260	280	300	330	350	370	400	425	440	460	480	500
PPO2 @1	14	13	12	11	10	10	9	8	8	7	7	7	7	6	6
PPO2 @1.3	17	17	15	14	13	12	11	11	10	9	9	9	8	8	8
PPO2 @1.4	19	18	17	15	14	13	12	12	11	10	10	9	9	9	8
PPO2 @1.5	20	19	18	17	15	14	13	12	12	11	10	10	10	9	9
PPO2 @1.6	21	21	19	18	16	15	14	13	13	12	11	11	10	10	9
END 100FT PPO2 @1	14/45	13/48	12/52	11/57	10/61	10/66	9/71	8/74	8/77	7/81	7/83	7/85	7/87	6/89	6/90
END 100 FT PPO2 @ 1.3	17/45	17/48	15/52	14/57	13/61	12/66	11/71	11/74	10/77	9/81	9/83	9/85	8/87	8/89	8/90
END 100 FT PPO2 @ 1.4	19/45	18/48	17/52	15/57	14/61	13/66	12/71	12/74	11/77	10/81	10/83	9/85	9/87	9/89	8/90
END 100 FT PPO2 @ 1.6	21/45	21/48	19/52	18/57	16/61	15/66	14/71	13/74	13/77	12/81	11/83	11/85	10/87	10/89	9/90
END 130FT PPO2 @1	14/33	13/36	12/41	11/45	10/49	10/54	9/60	8/64	8/67	7/72	7/75	7/77	7/79	6/81	6/83
END 130 FT PPO2 @ 1.3	17/33	17/36	15/41	14/45	13/49	12/54	11/60	11/64	10/67	9/72	9/75	9/77	8/79	8/81	8/83
END 130 FT PPO2 @ 1.4	19/33	18/36	17/41	15/45	14/49	13/54	12/60	12/64	11/67	10/72	10/75	9/77	9/79	9/81	8/83
END 130 FT PPO2 @ 1.6	21/33	21/36	19/41	18/45	16/49	15/54	14/60	13/64	13/67	12/72	11/75	11/77	10/79	10/81	9/83

Best gas meters

Best gas Chart Meters Created By Anton Swanepoel															
Depth Meters	18	21	24	27	30	33	36	39	42	45	48	51	54	57	60
PPO2 @1	35	32	29	27	25	23	21	20	19	18	17	16	15	15	14
PPO2 @1.3	46	42	38	35	32	30	27	26	25	23	22	21	20	19	18
PPO2 @1.4	50	45	41	38	35	32	29	28	27	25	24	23	22	21	20
PPO2 @1.5	53	48	44	40	37	35	32	30	29	27	26	24	23	22	21
PPO2 @1.6	57	51	47	43	40	37	34	32	31	29	27	26	25	24	23
END 30M PPO2 @1					25	23/7	21/15	20/19	19/23	18/28	17/31	16/35	15/38	15/41	14/43
END 30M PPO2 @ 1.3					32	30/7	27/15	26/19	25/23	23/28	22/31	21/35	20/38	19/41	18/43
END 30M PPO2 @ 1.4					35	32/7	29/15	28/19	27/23	25/28	24/31	23/35	22/38	21/41	20/43
END 30M PPO2 @ 1.6					40	37/7	34/15	32/19	31/23	29/28	27/31	26/35	25/38	24/41	23/43
END 39M PPO2 @1								20	19/6	18/11	17/16	16/20	15/24	15/26	14/30
END 39M PPO2 @ 1.3								26	25/6	23/11	22/16	21/20	20/24	19/26	18/30
END 39M PPO2 @ 1.4								28	27/6	25/11	24/16	23/20	22/24	21/26	20/30
END 39M PPO2 @ 1.6								32	31/6	29/11	27/16	26/20	25/24	24/26	23/30

Depth Meters	63	66	72	78	84	90	100	106	112	121	129	133	139	145	152
PPO2 @1	13	13	12	11	10	10	9	8	8	7	7	7	6	6	6
PPO2 @1.3	17	17	15	14	13	13	11	11	10	10	9	9	8	8	8
PPO2 @1.4	19	18	17	16	15	14	12	12	11	10	10	9	9	9	8
PPO2 @1.5	20	19	18	17	16	15	13	13	12	11	10	10	10	9	9
PPO2 @1.6	22	21	19	18	17	16	14	13	13	12	11	11	10	10	9
END 30M PPO2 @1	13/46	13/48	12/52	11/56	10/61	10/65	9/71	8/74	8/77	7/81	7/84	7/85	6/87	6/89	6/91
END 30M PPO2 @ 1.3	17/46	17/48	15/52	14/56	13/61	13/65	11/71	11/74	10/77	10/81	9/84	9/85	8/87	8/89	8/91
END 30M PPO2 @ 1.4	19/46	18/48	17/52	16/56	15/61	14/65	12/71	12/74	11/77	10/81	10/84	9/85	9/87	9/89	8/91
END 30M PPO2 @ 1.6	22/46	21/48	19/52	18/56	17/61	16/65	14/71	13/74	13/77	12/81	11/84	11/85	10/87	10/89	9/91
END 39M PPO2 @1	13/33	13/36	12/41	11/45	10/49	10/54	9/61	8/64	8/68	7/72	7/75	7/77	6/79	6/81	6/83
END 39M PPO2 @ 1.3	17/33	17/36	15/41	14/45	13/49	13/54	11/61	11/64	10/68	10/72	9/75	9/77	8/79	8/81	8/83
END 39M PPO2 @ 1.4	19/33	18/36	17/41	16/45	15/49	14/54	12/61	12/64	11/68	10/72	10/75	9/77	9/79	9/81	8/83
END 39M PPO2 @ 1.6	22/33	21/36	19/41	18/45	17/49	16/54	14/61	13/64	13/68	12/72	11/75	11/77	10/79	10/81	9/83

Quick Reference

EAD ft formula:

$$\frac{(1 - FO2) * (Depth + 33)}{0.79} - 33$$

EAD m formula:

$$\frac{(1 - FO2) * (Depth + 10)}{0.79} - 10$$

Pressure T formula :

Pg = Fg * Pd

In short

Pg = Fg * Pd
Fg = Pg / Pd
Pd = Pg / Fg

Need O2 Formula :

FO2 * Fill pressure

O2 to add formula

((Want Fg – Fill Fg) / Fg of nitrogen in fill mix) * fill pressure

Left over O2 formula:

Left over pressure * FG in tank

Still need O2 formula:

Total O2 Needed – Left over O2 in tank

Add O2% of fill pressure formula:

O2 pressure / pressure left to fill

Oxygen needed to add = ((want percentage - Top up O2 : percentage) / nitrogen percentage in top up mix) * fill pressure

O2% needed at depth formula:
Pressure at depth * FG

Pressure at depth formula:
(Depth ft / 33) + 1
(Depth m/ 10) + 1

END N2 only formula:
$$\frac{\text{Pnd} * 0.79}{\text{Ptd}}$$

END O2 + N2 only formula:
Pnd / Ptd

Helium narcosis ft formula:
Narcosis for He = (0.235 * he% * total ata * 33) - 33

Helium narcosis m formula:
Narcosis for He = (0.235 * He% * total ata * 10) - 10

Helium need formula
FHe * fill pressure

Actual Helium needed formula:
He pressure needed * FHe in tank

O2 in He tank formula:
FO2 * He fill pressure

New Helium percentage formula:
$$\frac{((\text{loop}\% - \text{O2}\%) * \text{original He}\%)}{(\text{original He}\% + \text{original Nitrogen}\%)}$$

New N2 percentage formula:
100 – (New O2% + New He%)

Free liter pressure to gas amount formula:
Cylinder size * fill pressure

Gas volume formula:
$$\frac{\text{Fill pressure}}{\text{Service pressure}} \times \text{Cylinder size}$$

Free liter to pressure formula:
Gas amount / Cylinder size

Cylinder size to pressure formula:
$$\frac{\text{Gas amount}}{\text{Cylinder size}} \times \text{Service rating}$$

Degrees Celsius to Degrees Fahrenheit formula:
$$\frac{°C \times 9}{5} + 32 = °F$$

Degrees Fahrenheit to Degrees Celsius formula:
$$\frac{(°F - 32) \times 5}{9} = °C$$

or

Degrees Celsius to Degrees Fahrenheit formula:
(°C * 1.8) + 32 = °F

Degrees Fahrenheit to Degrees Celsius formula:
(°F – 32) / 1.8 = °C

1 Bar = 14.503774 psi

(Bar is a measurement unit of pressure and is equal to 1,000,000 dynes per square centimeter (baryes), or 100,000 Newton per square meter (Pascal)).

(Pound per square inch (psi, lbf/in^2 or lbf/in^2) is a unit of pressure or stress based on avoirdupois units, and is the pressure resulting from a force of one pound-force applied to an area of one square inch).

1 pascal = 0.000145037738007 psi, or 1.0E-5 bar
(pascal is the SI derived unit for pressure)

10 msw = 32.81 ft: 10 fsw = 3.048 msw

End Note

Thank you for your purchase of this book. May it be a constant companion and an old friend on your journeys.

Happy blending and safe diving.

For comments please e-mail me at antonswanepoel@yahoo.com
For bulk purchases and discount for resellers, please e-mail info@antonswanepoelbooks.com

Anton Swanepoel

For More information and free sample downloads of other books by me, including news on books currently in progress visit www.antonswanepoelbooks.com
Be sure to check out the free stuff page that is loaded with free books from writing tips, weight loss, health tips and more.

Resources

Resources include but are not limited to:

Books:
Technical Diver Encyclopedia
Technical Diving From The Bottom Up
Deep Deeper Deepest
Mixed Gas Diving
Diving Physiology In Plain English
Exploration And Mixed Gas Diving
Deeper Diving

People:
Barry Neal Coleman
Donald R. Shirely
Tom Mount

Spelling and grammar:
Toni McNally
Ginger It! Software
WhiteSmoke 2011+ software

Internet websites:
http://en.wikipedia.org
http://www.ehow.com
http://www.dictionary.com
http://www.convertunits.com

Other Books by this Author

For a complete list of books by the author and more details on each book see
www.antonswanepoelbooks.com/books.php

Taking on the Road, Two Wheels at a Time

www.antonswanepoelbooks.com/taking_on_the_road.php

Traveling by motorcycle is far different than any other means of transport. In a car, you are always a passenger, seeing a movie of the road going by. On a bike you become one with it, the road and your surrounding is no longer a movie, it's a part of you. For you feel every corner, every bump and your body flexes in harmony with the bike's suspension. You smell the flowers, earth and rain, feel the wind and hear birds as you go, *you are alive*.

This book aims to help you prepare for your next adventure or your first, from down to the pub races, breakfast runs, multiple weeklong rallies, or yearlong multi country travel. From gear selection, packing right, understanding your bike and setting the suspension right to maintenance on the road.

The Art of Travel

www.antonswanepoelbooks.com/the_art_of_travel.php

Travelling is more than just reaching your destination; it's the journey in its totality. Travel is about growing as a person.

Pre-planning, gear selection, backpacks, tents, sleeping bags, boots, clothing, flashlights, GPS devices, pickpocketing, robbery, abduction, date rape drugs, protecting your food in the wild, keeping the crawlers out of your sleeping bag at night, and tips to help you with sticky situations along the way, are all covered in depth.

New adventures and friends are out there, what are you waiting for?

Gas Blender Program

www.antonswanepoelbooks.com/gas_blender_program.php

A step by step guide to creating your own gas blender program in Excel.

This book will show you how to write a blender program in Excel step by step with the values needed for every cell and function. No need to be a programmer, just type in the values from each step.

The program will run on most devices that support spreadsheets, from computers, laptops, smart phones, palms, and iPhones.
Calculations for Nitrox, Tri-Mix, Helair, Heliox, EAD and END are covered, in addition to calculations for actual rebreather loop at depth and END included.

Dive Computers

www.antonswanepoelbooks.com/dive_computers.php

The purpose and aim of this book is to help you in understanding how dive computers work, including calculations on decompression stops, deep stops, ascend ceilings, on- and off gassing, RGBM, VPM and gradient factors.

Sea and Motion Sickness

http://www.antonswanepoelbooks.com/motion_sickness.php

In this book, we will look at what motion sickness is, space sickness, virtual environment sickness, and sea sickness, their causes and triggers, with advice for preventing and treating them. Included in the book is ginger, antihistamine medication, wrist bands, natural herbs, behavior adaption and a lot more, all helping you travel without motion sickness.

Writing and Publishing Your Own Book

http://www.antonswanepoelbooks.com/writing_and_publishing.php

Change your words from 'I am going', to 'I have written a book'
You can be a writer, for it's a skill learnable by most people. Being a writer is not only a dream for the select few, it's within most people's ability.
In this book I will show you the steps to start and finish writing your book, including publishing and selling it. If you already have books written, you can use the tips to enhance old books and improve future books.

Deep and safety Stops, including Ascent speed and Gradient Factors

http://www.antonswanepoelbooks.com/deepstops.php

This book looks at the research done and current understandings of deep stops, both for and against deep stops. The book's aim is not to advocate or discredit the use of deep stops, but rather to be neutral and provide the reader with the most up to date knowledge, research and methods used by various groups, from military to recreational diving. The reader is shown the risks of both incorporating deep stops or not into their dive profile and it is up to the reader to decide if using deep stops is of any benefit in addition to how if any the user will calculate and execute those stops.

This book also looks at safety stops, ascent speed, descent speed, oxygen window and gradient factors and how they affect your decompression schedule

Ear Pain

http://www.antonswanepoelbooks.com/ear_pain.php

There are a few different causes of ear pain, and the treatment for each may differ. Understanding why your ears hurt is the first step in finding the off switch to the pain and preventing it from coming on again. Some of the topics covered are: ear pain due to barotrauma, swimmer's ear, surfer's ear, jogging and waterskiing, cold in the ear, airplane ear, ear infection, Tinnitus and referred pain from a tooth abscess. From causes, prevention, to treatment in detail. Additional included is over 10 ways to equalize your ears.

See www.antonswanepoelbooks.com for releases not listed here.

Made in the USA
San Bernardino, CA
07 February 2014